Niche Strategies for Downtown Revitalization

A hands-on guide to developing, strengthening and marketing niches

Written by
N. David Milder

Published by
**Downtown Research
& Development Center
215 Park Avenue South – Suite 1301
New York, NY 10003
(212) 228-0246**

Library of Congress Catalog Card Number: 97-65110
ISBN 0-915910-40-3

CONTENTS

LIST OF TABLES

LIST OF FIGURES

ABOUT THE AUTHOR

N. David Milder has been using his market research skills to develop effective public policies and to help revitalize urban commercial districts, including downtowns, for more than 20 years.

Since 1977, Milder has been operating DANTH, Inc., a consulting firm specializing in developing recruitment programs, databases, comprehensive retail revitalization strategies, economic development strategies, market analyses and technical assistance programs for clients like the City of Charlotte, NC, the Englewood [NJ] Economic Development Corporation, the Incorporated Village of Garden City, NY, The Rutland [VT] Partnership, the Grand Central Partnership in Manhattan, the Ohio Department of Economic and Community Development and Forest City Development in CA, and has developed training programs for Main Street New Jersey and the Massachusetts Executive Office of Community and Economic Development, among others.

Previously, Milder has published numerous technical reports and two monographs (*Municipal Service Districts in North Carolina* and *Tools and Techniques for Financing Downtown Revitalization*), as well as articles in such journals as *Urban Land*, *The City Almanac* and *Comparative Political Studies*.

PREFACE

Across the continent, there are literally thousands of businessmen, property owners, developers, government officials, concerned residents, consultants, district managers and other specialists who are striving to improve their downtowns. One of my major objectives in writing this book is to share with them some of the knowledge I have accumulated over the past 20 years concerning the use of niches to formulate and implement successful downtown revitalization strategies. I also hope that the discussion will engender in readers some of my spirited enthusiasm for the niche approach, which is invariably successful when it is used correctly.

Niche strategies are, as a rule, conceptually simple and therefore clear and easy to communicate. Often, when niche strategies are presented they are perceived by the audience to be full of common sense — a sure sign that the strategy will succeed. Niche strategies also provide an immediate focus to revitalization efforts. Many downtown organizations — especially new ones — lack such a focus. Consequently, niche strategies customarily lead to a more efficient and effective use of scarce organizational resources, such as money and personnel. Another attractive characteristic of niche strategies is that their use has a kind of internal logic (to be explained in Chapter 5) that stimulates downtown businesses to engage in organized, concerted activities.

Obviously, a book of this size imposes some limits, so I have not tried to make the reader an immediate expert in the creation and use of niche-based downtown revitalization strategies. But I do hope that this book will give readers an introduction that is strong enough to enable them to immediately begin to use the niche concept in their daily business, government and professional activities. It is my hope that this book will also enable readers to deal in a more informed manner with downtown specialists — market researchers, business recruiters, events coordinators, and so on — whom they may want to work with in developing and using downtown niche strategies.

I have made a considerable effort to include examples of niches in downtowns of diverse sizes from all parts of the United States. However, given the fact that most of my professional work has occurred in the northeastern region of the United States, and especially in the New York-New Jersey-

Connecticut metropolitan region, I hope the reader will understand my somewhat disproportionate use of case studies from downtowns in this part of America. Since I am always interested in learning about new niches, I do invite readers to send me information about successful niches in downtowns that I have not mentioned.

Space does not permit me to acknowledge here all the people who either taught me directly or gave me the opportunities to learn on my own about niches and downtown revitalization. Certainly my family, especially my wife Laura and my recently deceased mother, rank high among them. I would like to give special mention to Larry Alexander, Bill Shore, Phil Burgess, Dick Anderson, Dick Courcelle and Peter Beronio. I also would like to acknowledge David Burkhalter, a great city manager, who brought me to Charlotte, NC and thus provided me with a wonderful opportunity to become interested in downtown revitalization. Finally, many thanks to Mary Barr who edited my manuscript with considerable skill, gave me needed feedback as I wrote, and, most importantly, helped me to clarify thoughts at several important junctures.

CHAPTER 1
INTRODUCTION

Downtowns, Darwin and Functional Paranoia

Astute downtown leaders know that they operate in a very competitive economic environment, one which is governed in a very Darwinian survival of the fittest. And within this very competitive environment, it is probably wise to assume that, even as your downtown copes with one strong competitive challenge, another will quickly follow. For example, immediately after World War II, downtowns began to suffer from an enormous population flight to the suburbs. Soon thereafter they were challenged even more by the newly invented suburban shopping malls. Years later, street-level downtown merchants often had to deal with malls that were being built in their own downtowns. Then, downtown merchants were adversely affected by the growth of catalog shopping, off-price centers and manufacturers' outlet centers. More recently, downtown merchants have had to cope with the "900-lb. retail gorillas," that is, big discounters, category killers and big box retailers. Next, they will probably have to contend with the impacts of retailing over the Internet where shoppers, using their computers, will be able to visit and make purchases at "virtual" stores.

Competition and Downtown Niches

Niche strategies are particularly well-suited for dealing with such a highly competitive situation and this book intends to improve the capabilities of downtown leaders to formulate and implement them. Most successful downtowns have been built upon the strengths of at least two or three economic niches. The more niches a downtown has, the more reasons it provides for people to visit and the greater the likelihood that their trips downtown will be multi-purpose. Being able to provide a compact and easily walkable venue for multi-purpose trips is what gives a downtown its true competitive advantage over shopping centers and malls.

Niche development and maintenance are forms of economic specialization. If downtowns must continually face some kind of 900-lb. retail gorilla, then a niche analysis can identify the parts of the bed the gorilla isn't sleeping on — in other words, those areas in which downtowns can become dominant. A good niche analysis can also unearth existing niches and identify ways in which they can become stronger.

A niche can be defined as a special market segment. Niches can be based on many things:

- a particular group of customers, such as office workers, the elderly or Latinos

- a specific kind of goods or services, such as children's clothing, furniture and home furnishings, food-for-the-home or entertainment

- a specific shopping environment — malls have been very successful in this regard, but so have places such as Soho[1] in New York City and South Beach in Miami Beach

While niches are usually considered within the context of consumers and retailing, there are also industrial niches and niches in the office space market (for example, back offices, headquarters, regional and district offices, county seat functions, etc.).

In discussing niches, it is often helpful to differentiate between:

- *Potential niches* in which a market opportunity exists, but a significant number of downtown businesses have not yet emerged

- *Existing unorganized niches* in which a significant number of downtown businesses have emerged, but do not act together

- *Existing organized niches* in which a significant number of downtown businesses have emerged and have joined together on advertising, promotional and business recruitment efforts

A proper analysis can use the niche concept to identify currently unmet market demands (potential niches) of both consumers and tenant prospects for downtown commercial space. Downtown organizations can take advantage of such information to attract businesses capable of responding to these needs.

For example, in downtown White Plains, NY, an analysis showed that local retailers had not responded to a significant amount of consumer demand for specialty foods. The niche-based retail revitalization strategy formulated for this downtown consequently recommended recruiting more specialty foods retail chains. It also recommended that the downtown organization bring these specialty food shops together to conduct cooperative advertising and joint promotions.

Niches...
• They are based on specialization;
• They focus on a part of a market;
• Are best when you can be unique, with little or no competition;
• A successful downtown has many "niches," so it can support multi-purpose visits.

Figure 1.1

Some Examples Of Downtown Niches
• Downtown Englewood: the home design and refurbishing center
• Bergenline Avenue: the children's wear and Hispanic niches
• Rutland Center: food-for-the-home, "weddings" and entertainment niches
• Hay-on-Wye (UK): second-hand book-store niche

Figure 1.2

The ideal downtown niche not only provides growth potential, but also an opportunity for the downtown to *dominate a particular market*. This is most likely to occur in economic areas in which the downtown has a comparative competitive advantage. Such a competitive advantage can be based on a variety of factors, though proximity to specific types of customers (for example, office workers or nearby residents) is perhaps the most basic. The people who live in and around a downtown, combined with the people who work there, have an extraordinary impact on its image and economic activity simply because they visit the downtown so frequently.

Yet downtown revitalization organizations often either ignore or are quite ignorant about these crucial consumer groups and the niche markets they can support. For example, a recent study of a community in Long Island, NY found that about 62 percent of the local household expenditures for groceries were being "exported" outside of the community. It also found that about $14.8 million of the approximately $32 million that local residents and office workers spend on dining out was being lost to eating and drinking establishments in other communities.[2]

Dominance is easiest to achieve from the perspectives of both business recruitment and attracting more consumers when the downtown already has a group of shops that are currently operating in the same retail function and are either already strong, or at least potentially capable of becoming strong. For example, there are 12 children's clothing shops that comprise an unorganized niche on Bergenline Avenue in West New York, NJ. These shops draw more shoppers to the area than any other group of shops in the area. When a downtown niche, such as this one, has many attractive shops in it, it can potentially serve as a specialized shopping center, capable of providing the consumer with a large selection of merchandise and prices within its specialized area. It becomes a true downtown destination. Consequently, such strong niches can draw customers from a fairly wide geographic area. But most often, such niches are not organized and do not engage in joint promotions, advertising or business recruitment. Consequently, they are not as strong or dominant as they could be.

All too frequently, downtown business operators do not know that such an unorganized niche even exists. For example, leaders in one New Jersey downtown did not know that they had over 35 shops in a furniture and home furnishings niche.

Sometimes, the shops in a strong existing downtown niche are located very close together. The "home lighting" district in lower Manhattan is a good example of this. Such proximity produces a "cluster" which is attractive to consumers because it makes it easy to comparison shop by strolling from store to store. Clusters have been the basis of revitalization strategies proposed for a number of downtowns, such as Danbury, CT and Boise, ID.[3]

By enabling merchants to organize and act in concert, a niche strategy can be used to make downtown retailers far more competitive than they would be if they acted alone. For example, downtown shops in a niche, even one of modest size, can band together in a joint advertising and promotional campaign. Together, they have the resources for a campaign that would be beyond what each could individually afford. And, together, they are able to project a more solid and robust image that instills in the consumer the impression of a broad selection of merchandise. This promotional tactic is often used by clusters of antique and crafts shops such as downtown Red Bank, NJ's jewelry niche and downtown Rutland, VT's wedding niche.

Niches can also be used as an effective business recruitment tool. As real estate brokers are fond of saying, "retailers are like sheep," and the existence of a niche demonstrates a proven level of customer traffic and expenditures. Strong existing niches can be used to recruit complementary firms. For example, the proven power of children's clothing shops to attract customer traffic may stimulate not only the interest of other children's clothing shops, but also of retailers selling toys, computer training services for youngsters and women's clothing (after all, who buys most of the children's clothing?). In downtown Englewood, NJ, the special improvement district is busily recruiting retailers who have the merchandise and services needed to round out its home center and women's specialty clothing niches.

A niche strategy can also provide a basis for concerted action among a large number of businesses that previously had been thought of as having nothing in common. For example, in downtown Rutland the "wedding niche" has been able to bring together travel agents, florists, printers, men's and women's clothing stores, jewelers, restaurants, caterers, etc., in one advertising and promotional campaign.

Niches and Downtown Organizations

The identification of potential niches and their development into a vibrant array of downtown businesses is a task well-suited for downtown districts and their management organizations. But many, if not most, downtowns have not performed the kind of quality market research that is needed to identify potential niches. Consequently, they are missing many significant growth opportunities. In some instances, this is the result of a mistaken adherence to the "if we build it they will come" dictum. In other instances, it is because downtown leaders believe that they know from their own experiences and observations all the market information they could ever possibly need. In still other instances, budgetary constraints leave no funds for market research or there are so few funds that work is done in a quick-and-dirty, "back of the envelope" manner.

Most existing downtown niches have just emerged "voluntarily," much like wild flowers in a garden, and are unorganized. Again downtown districts and their management organizations can be an important mechanism for strengthening each unorganized niche by helping its members to join together and by providing the management umbrella for niche advertising, promotions and recruitment programs. But, here again, many downtown leaders do not know how to go about "organizing" their existing niches, or they just may not understand the powerful results they can achieve by doing so.

Objectives

In the chapters to follow, readers will be provided with information that will enable them to:

- Understand what niches are.

- Be familiar with some of the more important national and regional trends that shape the emergence of potential niches.

- Identify their downtowns' potential niches.

- Understand some of the constraints on the development of particular niches that affect their feasibility in each downtown.

- Identify their own existing, but unrecognized downtown niches.

- Develop niche-based consumer-oriented advertising and promotional campaigns.

- Develop niche-based business recruitment campaigns.

CHAPTER 2
TYPES OF NICHES

Looking at the niches various downtowns across the country have developed over the past 20 years reveals not only that they are numerous, but that they are very rich in their diversity. There is probably no better way for someone to become familiar with the concept of niches and to learn what to look for in their downtown than by taking a quick tour of some existing downtown niches in other cities.

Consumer-Based Retail Niches

Some niches are based on consumer groups, who may utilize a wide range of goods and services:

1. *Ethnic Groups.* Nationally, African Americans, Asians and especially Latinos are becoming increasingly important to retailers because they account for 70 percent of the nation's population growth. They now have an annual buying power of about $660 billion.[4] Experts believe that savvy retailers could substantially increase their sales, if they knew how to sell to these minority groups.

> **Ethnic Retail Markets Are Huge**
> - Nationally, ethnic minorities generate about $660 billion in annual buying power
> - They now account for 70% of the nation's population growth
> - Many retailers could increase their sales by 36% to 42% if they knew how to sell to these groups

Figure 2.1

Many downtowns across the continent have been enlivened by becoming major activity centers for one or more ethnic groups. Often these ethnic groups are considered as poor minorities, but because of their sheer number and concentration, they can have enormous spending power. These groups also can bring so much pedestrian activity downtown that one former president of Bloomingdale's called these ethnic downtowns "retail beehives."

For many years, downtown organizations ignored these ethnic groups, preferring to attempt to draw back middle-class, white shoppers who had moved to the suburbs. But clever downtown leaders have recognized the value of these ethnic markets. Here are some examples of downtowns that have successfully captured ethnic niche markets:

- *Downtown Brooklyn*. Fulton Mall in this downtown is a predominantly African-American shopping area. With approximately two million square feet (SF) of retail space and more than 350 stores anchored by such major chains as Macy's and Toys 'R' Us, this mall had sales estimated at $450 million in 1995. Retail rents are in the $75/SF–$100/SF range. Merchant profit margins on the mall are reportedly higher than on some of Midtown Manhattan's most chic retail streets.

  Jamaica Center in Queens is another important African-American retail center in the NY-NJ-CT metropolitan region, with annual sales of about $184 million.

- *Bergenline Avenue, West New York, NJ*. This linear commercial strip is the downtown for a community of about 46,000 people. It has about 320 shops and 700,000 SF of retail space. In 1995, it had total retail sales estimated at $125 million. It has become a major Latino shopping area, initially stimulated by Cuban immigrants, but more recently attracting significant numbers of Dominicans, Colombians, Mexicans and people from El Salvador. While most shoppers come from the nearby "core" trade area, many Latino customers are attracted from other parts of Hudson County as well as parts of Bergen County and Manhattan.

  Fordham Road and the Hub in the Bronx are two other Latino-based shopping areas in the NY-NJ-CT metropolitan region. They had annual sales estimated to be between $180 million and $280 million in 1995.

- *Downtown Miami*. This downtown has parlayed its geographic location and Cuban population into becoming the major financial center for American and European firms interested in doing business in Latin America as well as for Latin American firms interested in penetrating American markets.

- *Main Street in Flushing, Queens, NY*. This once-struggling neighborhood downtown has become a major Chinese-American business center that now offices more than 1,000 foreign firms. It also has a new Sheraton Hotel that was financed with funds from Taiwanese business interests. Many national retail chains such as Stern's, Caldor's, Barnes & Noble, etc., have also been drawn to this vibrant commercial center.

The downtown has numerous restaurants, and positive reviews in *The New York Times* have aided their success in drawing significant numbers of non-Chinese, "crossover" diners.

- *Cedar Lane in Teaneck, NJ.* This "Main Street"-type shopping area has a significant number of shops and restaurants that target the tastes and needs of Orthodox Jewish consumers. According to one source, who cites congregational records as his evidence, there are about 1,200 Orthodox Jewish households in Teaneck, which is about nine percent of all Teaneck households. Another source, a business operator who says he performed his own market research, claims there are now 1,700 Orthodox households, which would be about 12.8 percent of all Teaneck households. Retailers in this niche do attract Orthodox Jewish customers from other communities in the region, but many of these business operators readily acknowledge that to be economically viable, they must attract "crossover" shoppers who are either non-Orthodox Jews or persons who are not even Jewish.

Downtown strategies formulated to develop an ethnic niche often should take into consideration the fact that some groups are far less homogeneous than is commonly thought. Among Latinos, for example, there are significant cultural differences among Dominicans, Mexicans, Colombians, Chileans, Brazilians, etc. These differences are demonstrated by a supermarket in Union City, NJ called *Mi Bandera*, in which the store has separate shelves for the merchandise particular to each Latin American nation. Similarly, there are substantial cultural differences between African Americans born in the United States and those coming from the islands in the Caribbean.

2. *Age Niches.* Many downtowns are becoming more attuned to age demographics and are targeting themselves to dominant age categories in their regions. Some of the more prevalent age niches are those targeting seniors and the youth market.

a) *Youth Niches.* For many years, downtown leaders only had a negative interest in age niches. They were concerned that their commercial area did not become a "hang-out" for teenagers, gangs or truants. But the teenage market has been gaining an increasingly significant amount of spending power: an estimated $109 billion nationally in 1995.[5]

In some downtowns located in or near colleges or universities, merchants have targeted college students and their success has varied:

- On Boston, MA's Newberry and Boyleston Streets, in Cambridge, MA's Harvard Square and along lower Broadway in Manhattan, retailers and restaurant owners have been very successful in attracting a strong college student clientele. University of Vermont students are one of the main reasons for the success of the Church Street pedestrian mall in Burlington, VT.

- In less urban locations such as Ithaca, NY and State College, PA, downtown merchants have been less successful in attracting college student dollars.

- Downtowns that have tried to target colleges whose students are primarily commuters, such as downtown Brooklyn, NY and Teaneck, NJ, have generally not had much success.

b) *Retiree niche.* Only in recent years have downtowns become aware of the value of the retiree niche.[6] And with 20 million Americans projected to retire in the coming decade, the attractiveness of this niche for downtowns can only be expected to grow. Many smaller downtowns and Main Streets have developed this niche. Hendersonville and Black Mountain, NC and Hot Springs, AR have known for decades that the retirees they attract contribute significantly to downtown merchant revenues. A study performed at the University of Jacksonville in Florida shows that each retired couple a community attracts can be expected to bring with them about $35,000 in annual income and $250,000 in savings. The study estimated that in terms of economic impact, each retiree was worth about 3.7 factory jobs. As one observer stated:

> "Retirees spend all their money locally, love to have their hair done, and eat out as often as they can. Many towns would rather have them than a factory."

The impact of retirees on a downtown is illustrated by what happened in Hindersonville, AL and Squim, WA:

- It is estimated that the retirees in Hindersonville receive over $117 million in Social Security benefits annually and that most of these funds are spent in downtown service-oriented businesses.

- In Squim, there were only eight restaurants 20 years ago before the town started to try to attract retirees. Today, it has more than 37.

3. *Tourists*. Tourism is becoming an increasingly important niche for downtowns all across the continent. In many instances, it is already a key source of downtown retail and entertainment revenues. In other instances, it is providing key market support for growth and revitalization. For example:

- Tourism is one of the keys to the revitalization of the South Beach area in Miami Beach, FL.

- It is also a key engine driving the revitalization of the 42nd Street-Times Square area in Manhattan. The Walt Disney Company and Livent, a Canadian theater developer and operator, will renovate major legitimate theaters and produce shows. A 75,000-SF Virgin Megastore has opened that sells music, books, movies and multimedia products and has a café and the only entrance to a four-screen Sony movie theater. American Multi-Cinemas has announced its intention to build a 150,000-SF 25-screen theater.

- Tourism is a fundamental component of Philadelphia, PA's economic revitalization strategy. The Pennsylvania Convention Center, Reading Terminal Market, famous restaurants such as Le Bec-Fin, major hotels such as the Bellevue, as well as 30 museum/cultural institutions and 13 theaters for the performing arts mean that the downtown's Center City Business Improvement District is a major player in implementing this strategy. The district now attracts 7.9 million visitors annually, of which 355,000 are conventioneers. The city also has just unrolled a $12-million tourism marketing campaign.

- Tourism is a prime potential market that downtown Rutland, VT plans to tap to support its future growth; it has already helped to make the Church Street Mall in Burlington, VT a success.

- The Chicago Place Mall in downtown Chicago, IL reports that visitors account for 45 percent of that center's annual sales.[7]

- The South Street Seaport in Manhattan reports that tourists account for 45 percent of its shoppers.[8]

- Tourists drawn to the Rock & Roll Hall of Fame in Cleveland, OH are spending significant amounts of money in downtown shops and restaurants.

The amount of money tourism can generate for downtown businesses is impressive. For example:

- Within a 15-minute walk of the intersection of Madison Avenue and 48th Street in Manhattan are 69 major hotels and clubs with a total of 28,307 rooms. The international tourists staying in hotels located within a 15-minute walk of Madison Avenue and 48th Street spent an estimated $305 million in New York retail shops in 1993. Some major retailers report that sales to shoppers who live anywhere beyond the New York metropolitan area account for 25–35 percent of their business.[9]

- The 1,050,000 international visitors to the Empire State Building in 1993 spent an estimated $237.6 million in New York retail shops.[10]

- Of the overseas visitors to New York City in 1993, 85 percent went shopping, 71 percent dined out in restaurants, 48 percent visited art galleries and museums, and 31 percent attended a concert, play or musical event.[11]

- Many downtown retail complexes report that tourists spend more per shopping trip than local customers. Horton Plaza in downtown San Diego, for example, found that tourists spend on average $73.31 each time they visited, compared to the $47.96 spent by local shoppers.[12]

- People attending downtown conventions in Philadelphia's Center City District had an estimated economic impact of $194 million in 1994.

- Tourism represents a potential market of at least $113 million for restaurants and retail shops in downtown Rutland, VT (pop. 18,000).[13]

Tourism once was an important factor to downtowns gifted by a nearby natural attraction such as Niagara Falls or by wondrous buildings, major museums or famous symphony orchestras such as London, Paris or New York. Recently, however, many smaller and less naturally spectacular down-towns are learning how to develop tourism as a major factor in their revitalization. In Gonzalez, TX, a community with a population of about 7,000, downtown leaders have adopted a tourism-driven revitalization strategy that combines:

- an expanded central business district

- new visitor-oriented businesses

- re-creation of the town's original market square

- park and historic development

- greenways

- a river park[14]

Communities with restored old historic buildings can often use this asset to attract tourists. Charleston, SC, Savannah, GA, and Santa Fe, NM are examples of this occurring in cities of well-known historic significance. Cape May, NJ, a smaller beach resort town with about 4,300 permanent residents, is a good example of a lesser-known town that capitalized on its well-preserved architecture. In the early 1970s, Cape May was in bad economic shape, with the downtown full of "big, drafty Victorian buildings, which require high maintenance." But in the mid-1970s, a significant revival of interest in Victoriana occurred, changing the former "white elephants" into attractive and successful B&Bs and hotels. Once a momentum for revitalization was built, Cape May became a National Historic Landmark, which in turn helped galvanize support in the town for future revitalization activities. Now, Cape May has reclaimed its traditional market of tourists from Philadelphia, while adding a significant number of visitors from New York and Washington, D.C.[15]

Downtowns can use niches to go beyond the usual "chamber of commerce"-type responses to inquiries. How? By fostering the development of and by nurturing more specific goods and services-based niches such as restaurants, the arts, entertainment, convention centers and hotels, major league sports teams, etc. The arts, in particular, have become an increasingly powerful tool for attracting tourists, because large numbers of travelers are more interested in "an art museum or music festival than a shopping district or theme park."[16] And the arts can be an important tourist generator even in smaller communities. For example, Jonesborough, TN, a community with a population of about 3,100, generated 8,600 visitors and $5 million in revenue from a storytelling festival.[17]

Mall operators are becoming increasingly involved in directly promoting and marketing their retail centers to tourists and this may be yet another area in which downtowners can learn from the malls. This will be discussed in greater detail in Chapter 5.

4. *The Office Worker Retail Niche.* This niche was the prime engine driving most downtown retail revitalization strategies during the 1980s. Since then, the nature of the office market has changed and continues to change, but office workers still remain a critical niche for downtown retailers. For example:

- A retail shop located in Manhattan at the intersection of 45th Street and Madison Avenue will be able to tap employees within a 2,253-ft. walking distance.[18] Such a store could easily tap the 194,910 people working in 137 Class A office buildings in the primary office worker trade area plus another 83,533 from the rest of Midtown. These 278,443 employees represent 63.1 percent of all Midtown office workers, and they spent about $759.8 million per year on workday retail items and food in 1995.[19]

- In downtown White Plains, there were between 19,750 and 21,004 office workers in November 1994 and they had a retail expenditure potential between $36.34 million and $38.06 million.[20]

When considering the office worker niche, it is important to keep in mind that most are clerical workers with modest incomes, who are not "quiche and Chablis" shoppers. Moreover, they tend to make big ticket purchases at shopping centers close to their homes. Their most frequent downtown purchases, besides food, are likely to be such items as greeting cards, books, tapes and CDs, etc. (see Table 2.1).

5. *Artists and Crafters.* The success of the Soho[21] area in lower Manhattan has encouraged a growing number of

The Kinds Of Merchandise Office Workers Will Shop For In Downtown White Plains			
Merchandise	Private Sector	Gov't.	WP Hospital
Greeting cards	86.1%	88.8%	57.8%
Books	65.3%	73.4%	43.2%
Shirts, blouses	61.8%	69.6%	44.1%
LPs, tapes,CDs	60.7%	65.8%	38.0%
Dress shoes	58.0%	66.7%	40.8%
Jeans, sweats	51.3%	57.1%	32.0%
China, pots, pans, etc.	46.6%	46.9%	33.7%
Jewelry	45.9%	46.9%	32.0%
Leather goods	44.2%	44.1%	28.7%
Athletic equip.	40.1%	42.1%	29.0%
Children's clothing	38.0%	43.0%	27.1%
Suits	37.2%	46.3%	30.9%
Electronic equipm't	30.9%	28.0%	17.7%
Food for home	30.4%	31.7%	36.0%
Prints, posters	24.6%	23.5%	15.4%
Major appliances	18.5%	19.9%	13.5%
Furniture	14.5%	17.8%	15.2%
N=	217	457	120

Table 2.1

downtowns to appreciate the importance of having artists and crafters live and work downtown. In Soho, artist live/work activity has attracted galleries, interesting restaurants and bars and off-beat, specialty retailers.

Artists tend to be "urban pioneers," attracted by low-cost, underutilized spaces in which they can both live and work — precisely the kind of spaces that are found in many downtowns. As two keen observers have noted:

"Artists, historically, have been attracted to underutilized buildings, choosing to live in them even when local regulations prohibit such use. In downtown revitalization efforts, artists tend to be among the most adaptable and adventurous of tenants. They are willing to live in conditions that others often find inconvenient or unacceptable."[22]

Eureka, CA has been suffering from a decline in the lumber and fishing industries, but the surrounding area is renowned for its beauty and has more artists per capita than any other county in California. Downtown leaders decided to take advantage of this valuable human resource and combine it with the downtown's underutilized, though attractive building stock by designing and marketing a cultural arts district. This involved a number of factors, including:[23]

- the passage of a municipal ordinance that would enable artists to live and work in the same downtown space

- a series of "phantom" galleries

- a $900,000 program to improve facades, signage and streetscapes

- recruitment of artists

- aggressive marketing of the district to artist-based businesses

Peekskill, NY, a small Hudson River community, also has had significant success in recruiting artists. Between 1991 and 1993, under a city-designed program, more than 50 artists from established arts communities in the New York City metropolitan region were convinced to move their studios and homes into 15 downtown buildings that had been especially renovated for them. As a consequence, downtown Peekskill has spawned seven galleries and exhibition spaces as well as a bookstore/espresso bar, book publishers, a marketing design firm, a frame shop, an interior design center, a gift shop and an art school. Older, established downtown merchants report an increase in business as a result of the city's artist recruitment program.[24]

Peekskill's program, like Eureka's, was multifaceted and included:

- a special zoning district

- low-interest renovation loans

- a marketing campaign

- weekly studio tours

- an art school

Niches Based on Goods and Services

Most retail and retail-related niches are based on the types of goods and services that downtown businesses and nonprofits offer. Some niches are based on retailers, others involve retailers and non-retailers, and still others involve only non-retailers.

1. *Home Furnishings Niche*. The Englewood Economic Development Corporation has concentrated its business recruitment efforts on three niches, one of which is focused on home furnishings. Englewood, NJ has a growing cluster of more than 30 shops in the areas of home remodeling, home furnishings and decorative design. Most of these shops are strong independents such as Eagle Paints, Mitchell Simon Hardware, Englewood Hardware, Wohner's Doors and Mantels, Michaelangelo's World of Marble, Goram Appliances, Habitat Kitchens, Rande Lynee Housewares, Star Carpets, Jordan Carpets, Lighting by Gregory, Crown House Antiques, Ophir Antiques and the Jewel Speigel Galleries. Recently, these were joined by Lechter's, Design Quest (a modern furniture store) and Englewood Design, Inc.

It is estimated that Englewood's home furnishings stores had sales of $21.2 million in 1993.[25] These shops draw customers from a primary trade area (Englewood and 11 adjacent towns) of 61,582 households that have an average income of $73,861 and an aggregate income of $4.5 billion. An analysis of the market area's lifestyles showed that there are more than 12,500 households now avidly engaged in home furnishing and decorating activities.

Many other downtowns either have a similar niche or have the potential to develop one. For example, just outside of downtown Dallas, there is a very strong furniture and home furnishings center. And, in the Soho section of Manhattan, a very strong home furnishings niche has developed around lower Broadway that includes such shops as Broadway Panhandler, Williams Sonoma, Knoll, Platypus, Portico Home and Pottery Barn.

2. *Antiques.* A few antique shops can be part of a larger furniture and home furnishings niche, but quite often downtowns will have so many that they constitute their own niche. This often happens in small and medium-sized communities, where antique sellers often form very strong symbiotic ties to the downtown's historical, crafts and hospitality niches. These downtowns show just how powerful a niche strategy can be for communities of this size.

For example, Waynesville, OH (population 1,950) claims to be the "Antiques Capital of the Midwest." Its "Old Main Street" historic district — five blocks of historic buildings, brick sidewalks, copper street lamps, flower boxes and street benches where people can rest or people-watch — is the location for more than 35 antique shops, including nine antique malls (see Table 2.2). Waynesville has had this antique niche for well over 25 years, though in recent years there has been a significant upgrading in the quality of the shops and the antiques. The antique niche has provided the foundation of customer traffic to support about 35 related specialty shops and art galleries. It also meshes well with the local hospitality niche, including the restored and redecorated Hammel House Inn, which was originally built in 1822 and served as an important stagecoach stop during the first half of the 1800s. On the outskirts of town is Pioneer Village, a restored group of 20 log houses that recreates pioneer life in the Caesar's Creek area during the 18th century.

Waynesville draws day-tripping antiquers from all over southwestern Ohio and tourists from across Ohio, Kentucky, Indiana and parts of Pennsylvania.[26] A substantial reason for this is Waynesville's location in the very scenic Little Miami River Valley. For thousands of years this valley was the home of powerful Indian tribes and later it became the scene of significant battles between natives and early white settlers. Fort Ancient State Park is famous for its mysterious burial mounds. Shakers were also attracted to the area.

Only 10 miles down the road from Waynesville is Lebanon, OH (population 10,500) which has over 30 antique shops (including seven malls) in and around its downtown area. Just as in Waynesville, these antique stores have provided a considerable customer base for about 30 art galleries, craft shops and specialty shops in the downtown area.

The Antique Niche In Waynesville, Ohio	
Firm Name	**Street**
Remember When Antiques	43 Main St
Miscellany Collection	49 S Main St
Shannondoah Antiques	55 S Main St
Bittersweet Antiques	57 S Main St
Velvet Bear Antiques	61 S Main St
Waynesville Antique Mall	69 S Main St
My Wife's Antiques	77 S Main St
Little Red Shed Antiques	85 S Main St
Olde Curiosity Shoppe	88 S Main St
Cranberry Corner Antiques	93 S Main St
Bakers Antiques	98 S Main St
Highlander House	22 S Main St
Brass Lantern Antiques	100 S Main St
Cheap Johns Country Store	100 S Main St
Hammel House Inn	121 S Main St
A Turn In Tyme	140 S Main St
Golden Pomegranata Antique Mall	140 S Main St
Khakis	195 S Main St
Crazy Quilt Antiques	211 S Main St
Stetson Place	234 S Main St
Back In The Barn	239-1/2 S Main St
Countree Accents	258 S Main St
Rose Cottage, The	258 S Main St
Tiffanys Treasures	273 S Main St
Spencers Antiques	278 S Main St
Cherry House	295 S Main St
Village Peddler, The	50 N Main St
My Favorite Shop	92 N Main St
Blueberry Hill Antiques & Collectibles	232 Miami St
Gingerbread And Olde Lace	244 South St
Silver City Mercantile Antiques	1555 E State Route
Southwest Images	1557 E State Route
High Street Antique Market	180 High St
Hearth & Home	234 High St
Augustines Emporium	260 High St
Hays Furniture	76 1st St
Source: SelectPhone 1996	

Table 2.2

Lebanon's antique niche also meshes nicely with other historical assets located in or around the downtown:

- The Warren County Historical Museum, which has the very impressive Robert and Virginia Jones Collection of Shaker furniture

- The Golden Lamb, Ohio's oldest inn and restaurant, which was built in 1803 and hosted 10 U.S. presidents; it is famous for the Shaker and Victorian furnishings in its guest rooms, which may be viewed when unoccupied

- Glendower State Memorial, a Greek revival mansion furnished with Ohio antiques

- The I&O Scenic Railway

The antique niches in Waynesville and Lebanon are coupled with smaller ones in nearby communities such as Mason, Springboro and Morrow. They combine to advertise themselves as "the highest concentration of antique shops in the USA." By agglomerating in this manner, they are better able to attract tourists from a multi-state geographic area. For example, one Waynesville antique dealer assured a potential out-of-state shopper that "there are at least three days of antiquing in the area" and "you'll need even more time if you want to really see everything."

Over the past three or four years an antique niche has also developed in downtown Carlisle, PA. This niche already has 24 shops and an annual antique show.

Larger downtowns, of course, can also develop antique niches: Philadelphia has developed one along Pine Street, as has Baltimore along Howard Street.

3. *Children's Wear.* The Bergenline Avenue shopping center in West New York, NJ has a very strong niche based on children's clothing and furniture. As can be seen in the table below, the 12 shops in this niche are the strongest reason trade area residents come to shop on Bergenline Avenue.

Many communities could not develop a children's wear niche in the past because nearby malls and shopping centers had department stores and national chains that dominated this market. The niche was able to grow on

Bergenline because the shops were mainly operated by Latinos who were targeting the heavily Latino local trade area. These shops, however, provide such a wide range of quality merchandise that they have been able to draw significant crossover traffic from non-Latino shoppers.

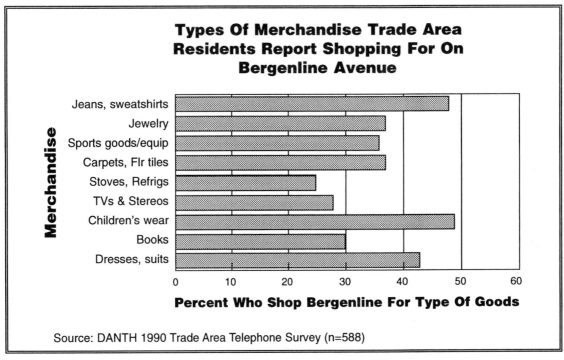

Figure 2.2

Recently, the prospects for downtowns developing a children's wear niche have greatly improved as chains such as Gap Kids, Guess for Kids, Toys 'R' Us and Kids 'R' Us have become much more interested in locating in downtown and Main Street-type locations.

Downtowns can develop a larger children's niche by combining stores focusing on children's clothing and furniture combined with computer-oriented ventures such as FutureKids, Technokids and Cyberstation, as well as operations focusing on martial arts and dancing. The latter, when located in storefronts, can be of additional value to a downtown because people tend to gather in a crowd to watch children go through their routines, much as crowds assemble outside the window of the Today Show's new studio in Rockefeller Center. Such crowds gather on Lincoln Mall in Miami Beach, FL, for example, to watch children taking classes at the Miami City Ballet.

4. *The Food-for-the-Home Niche.* If there is one retail function that any downtown or "Main Street" commercial center should capture, it is groceries. It should be a "captive" market in which local merchants can take the best advantage of their proximity to their potential customers. When a downtown is decimated by external competitors, this should be its "back-to-the-wall" niche on which it can base its revitalization because it can demonstrate that the downtown can still attract significant levels of customer traffic. Unfortunately, this market often seems so mundane or pedestrian that its importance is overlooked. But many downtowns in recent years, including Somerville, NJ, Great Neck Plaza, NY and Rutland, VT, have used new supermarkets to anchor their revitalization. White Plains, NY has been interested in attracting a supermarket to downtown, but has been unable to put together an appropriate site.

Figure 2.3

Often, food-for-the-home firms supply the type of merchandise on which core trade area residents feel most under-served. For example, a survey of people living in apartments along the "Gold Coast" on the Hudson River in

New Jersey found that the types of new stores they wanted the most were those selling fresh baked goods, fresh meats and fish and fresh fruits and vegetables (see Figure 2.3).

The importance of this market also is demonstrated by a recent study in Upperton, NY,[27] which found that:

- In Upperton and surrounding communities, respondents to a telephone survey reported that they shop for groceries about seven times a month.

- With Upperton having about 9,247 households that means a total of about 64,729 shopping trips per month. Based on the proportion of exported grocery expenditures (62 percent), it is estimated that Upperton residents are making 40,000 grocery shopping trips each month to other communities.

That is an enormous amount of shopping activity for a community to lose.

In downtown Rutland, VT, a new 58,000 SF Price Chopper is attracting more than 10,000 cars (and their shopping passengers) every Saturday and Sunday. It is the strongest supermarket in central Vermont and perhaps even the state, dwarfing its rivals in size and customer traffic. The Rutland Partnership's 1994 telephone survey found that Price Chopper had a 50 percent market share among respondents living within 10 miles of the downtown and a 25 percent share among those living between 11 and 20 miles away.[28]

Smart merchants are wanting to be close to Price Chopper, both geographically and in retail functions. Residents of downtown Rutland's trade area for GAFO[29] merchandise also shop frequently for groceries: 49 percent shop for groceries once a week, 22.8 percent twice a week, and 20.6 percent three or more times a week.[30]

Across the nation, supermarket chains are finding highly urban infill sites to be increasingly attractive because urban markets are relatively untapped, while those in the suburbs are often saturated. In many instances, the residential density near urban sites means that shoppers usually will walk to their supermarket, thus negating the need for large amounts of parking. Still, highly urban downtown sites often have significant problems with land acquisition, permits and approvals as well as high construction costs.[31] The fact that many supermarket chains nevertheless are interested in downtown sites reflects the size and strength of the consumer markets that the chains believe they can tap in these locations.

There are over 1,800 public — or farmers' — markets in the United States,[32] and they are another important mechanism for downtowns in carving out a substantial presence in the food-for-the-home niche. This fact is exemplified by:

- Pike Street Market in Seattle, WA

- Lexington Market in Baltimore, MD

- Reading Terminal Market in Philadelphia, PA

- the French Market in New Orleans, LA

- the Farmers' Market in Paterson, NJ

- the Farmers' Market in Carrboro, NC

- the Farmers' Market in Jamaica, NY

- the Farmers' Market in Winston-Salem, NC

While most of these markets serve local residents, some, such as Pike Street, Reading Terminal[33] and the French Market, have become important tourist destinations. Also, many of these public markets can become strong attractions for downtown office workers at lunch time; this has happened at the Reading Terminal Market, the Lexington Market and the Farmers' Market in Jamaica, NY.

An emerging trend is for upscale, specialty food chains (such as Dean and DeLuca, Sutton Place Gourmet and Fresh Fields) to be interested in downtown locations. Such shops can greatly enhance a downtown's strength in the food-for-the-home niche.

The importance of specialty food chains in this niche is shown by some recent market research done for White Plains, NY. Among residents surveyed who live within a seven- to 10-minute drive of the downtown (the trade area residents closest to downtown), between 25 and 30 percent said that the shops within a 10-minute drive of their homes selling deli items, fresh fruits and vegetables, fresh baked goods, fresh meats and fresh fish were "not good." This dissatisfaction provides a basis for developing high-quality specialty food stores in downtown White Plains. Core area residents spend about $76.9 million for these food products, so the expenditures of dissatisfied consumers amount to about $20.9 million (see Table 2.3).[34]

Market Potentials For Downtown White Plains In Specialty Foods

Specialty Food Items	Core Area Expenditure Potentials	Index of Consumer Dissatisfaction*	DT White Plains Growth Potential
Deli items	$ 5,400,000	0.265	$ 1,431,000
Fresh Fruits & Veg.	$ 19,730,000	0.272	$ 5,366,560
Fresh baked goods	$ 12,320,000	0.295	$ 3,634,400
Fresh meats	$ 20,180,000	0.302	$ 6,094,360
Fresh Seafood	$ 6,999,000	0.305	$ 2,134,695
Wines	$ 5,370,000	0.148	$ 794,760
Cheeses	$ 6,900,000	0.217	$ 1,497,300
Totals	$ 76,899,000	0.272	$ 20,953,075

* Source: DANTH Trade Area Telephone Survey 1994, Scan/US expenditure data

Table 2.3

Based on survey findings and an analysis of census data, it is possible to estimate that adults living within a seven- to 10-minute drive of downtown White Plains make about 830,000 grocery shopping trips each month. If the downtown street-level shops could develop a specialty foods niche, they could attract a lot more customer traffic, with a significant proportion occurring after 5 p.m.[35]

5. *Jewelry Niches*. Perhaps the most famous jewelry niche is located on 47th Street, between Fifth Avenue and the Avenue of the Americas in Manhattan. Within this very concentrated area is one of the largest and most important agglomerations of jewelry and jewelry-related firms in the world.

However, the oldest jewelry district in America is not in New York, but in downtown Philadelphia. The heart of this district is a true cluster of jewelry and jewelry-related firms located along one block of Sansom Street between 7th and 8th Streets. Within this district are more than 150 independent jewelry and jewelry-related firms, making it the second largest in the nation. These firms employ over 300 jewelers, designers, diamond cutters, goldsmiths, etc.

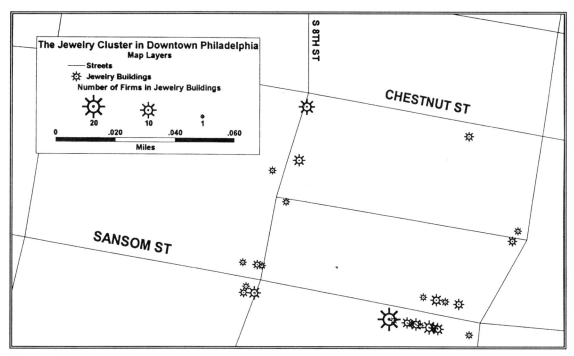

Figure 2.4

This jewelry niche is a very good example of a "cluster," that is, a geographic concentration of firms in a similar line of business (see Figure 2.4). Clusters can be powerful because they can act like specialized shopping centers.

The firms in downtown Philadelphia's jewelry district have taken advantage of their cluster to use brick pavers and banners to let shoppers know that they are on "Jewelers' Row."

Smaller downtowns can also have jewelry niches. In downtown Red Bank, NJ, for example, there are over 10 jewelry and jewelry-related firms.

6. *Arts and Entertainment Niches.* In cities large and small across the country, downtown revitalization efforts are being strengthened by the nurturing of arts and entertainment venues. By husbanding them, downtowns are able to bring significant levels of activity back to downtown streets at night and to improve their public image as interesting, attractive and safe places for people to live, work, shop and generally enjoy themselves. They are also a major means for downtowns to attract tourists and capture their dollars. These activities are quite broad, ranging from going to the movies, the theater, music concerts, dance concerts or ballets, to visiting museums and art galleries, going to craft shops, visiting nightclubs and dining out. Each of

these activities, in their own right, can constitute a viable niche, but they also are so mutually supportive of each other that together they can function as a single niche. Whether a downtown organization will want to treat them as separate niches or group them together as a single larger niche will depend on local market conditions and the organization's goals and capabilities.

Downtown White Plains provides a good example of the market opportunities downtowns can have in the arts and entertainment area. For many years, this downtown has not had a movie. It also has no museum, legitimate theater or concert hall. There are just two or three arts or crafts galleries.

How Often White Plains Trade Area Residents Engage In Leisure Time Activities

	__All__	__Area__			__Income__		
		__Core__	__Outer__	__<50k__	__50-75k__	__75-100k__	__100k+__
Activities In Past Month (mean)							
Go to restaurant for dinner	5.17	5.09	5.28	3.78	4.33	6.27	6.87
Go to a movie	1.07	1.02	1.12	0.79	1.27	1.21	1.34
Shopping for major items	3.20	3.38	2.96	2.67	3.69	3.36	4.12
Grocery shopping	8.02	7.80	8.30	7.16	7.99	7.88	8.78
Activities Over Past Year (mean)							
Go to major museum	2.80	2.87	2.70	1.29	3.43	2.69	4.48
Go to an art gallery	1.96	1.79	2.18	0.77	1.82	1.83	3.31
Attend music concert	3.14	2.85	3.52	1.94	2.55	4.62	3.93
Go to ballet/dance concert	0.88	0.99	0.73	0.38	1.19	1.27	1.15
Theatrical play	2.26	2.45	2.02	1.15	2.08	2.86	3.50
Visit crafts shop/gallery	3.29	2.90	3.79	1.98	3.18	4.12	4.22
Go to night club/cabaret	3.55	3.34	3.83	4.81	3.78	3.40	3.23
Activities Respondents Would Like To Do More Often (%)							
Go to museum	26%	28%	24%	24%	32%	27%	24%
Visit art gallery	17%	20%	13%	16%	19%	21%	19%
Go to music concert	29%	29%	30%	25%	37%	32%	27%
Go to dance event	16%	18%	13%	12%	20%	16%	17%
Go to a play	37%	43%	31%	35%	41%	40%	41%
Visit crafts shop	14%	16%	12%	10%	18%	15%	18%
Go to night club	19%	22%	14%	19%	24%	23%	19%
None of above	32%	28%	38%	32%	28%	19%	32%

Table 2.4

The population in White Plains' primary upscale trade area, according to a telephone survey, engages in arts- and entertainment-related activities with a good deal of frequency (see Table 2.4). Following is how many times, on average, survey respondents reported engaging in the following activities over the past year:

- going to the movies, 12.84

- going to a night club, 3.55

- visiting a crafts shop, 3.29

- attending a music concert, 3.14

- going to a major museum, 2.8

- going to a play, 2.26

- visiting an art gallery, 1.96

- going to a dance concert, 0.88

This would translate into the following number of admissions for adults in the trade area: movies 2,587,209; night clubs 715,311; crafts galleries 662,922; music concerts 632,697; major museums 564,189; plays 455,381; art galleries 394,932; and dance concerts 177,316. Moreover, 37 percent claimed that they would like to go to more plays than they now do, while 29 percent said the same about musical concerts and 26 percent made similar remarks about their museum attendance.[36]

The trade area survey also asked respondents an open-ended question about the types of activities they would like to be able to do more of in downtown White Plains. Significantly, only 9 percent said more shopping; another 9 percent said dining out. But 57 percent mentioned an arts and entertainment activity:

- going to a movie, 21%

- attending a play, concert or dance recital, 18%

- night life, 9%

- visiting an art gallery, 5%

- going to a museum, 4%

Activities Trade Area Residents Want To Do More Of In Downtown White Plains					
Activity	**All**	**Core**	**Outer**	**<$50k**	**$100k+**
Go to movies	21%	26%	15%	21%	25%
Go to play,concert,dance recital	18%	20%	15%	14%	25%
Go to art gallery	5%	5%	6%	3%	6%
Go to museum	4%	3%	5%	2%	5%
Shopping	9%	11%	8%	8%	13%
Dining out	9%	10%	7%	5%	13%
Night life	9%	10%	7%	14%	7%
Sports activities	8%	9%	7%	13%	7%
Children's activities	3%	3%	2%	4%	2%
Other	1%	1%	2%	1%	1%
Don't know/refused	34%	30%	39%	37%	28%

Table 2.5

The survey provides strong evidence about what activities downtown White Plains must nurture to ensure its future economic success. Residents in its primary trade area clearly would like to engage in more arts and entertainment activities in downtown White Plains. In response to this market situation, one developer has already announced a major retail project to be built in the heart of downtown, anchored around a 16-screen cinemaplex.

Arts and entertainment can provide important market opportunities even in smaller downtowns such as Rutland, VT. The Rutland Partnership's 1994 telephone survey found that the average resident can be expected to go to the movies about eight times a year and to attend a concert, play or other live performance about 1.7 times a year. It is estimated that all the households in the primary trade area will spend about $2.7 million on movie, theater, ballet, opera and "other" entertainment. Households in the $50,000-plus range spend twice as much on entertainment as the average household (such households in downtown White Plains' primary trade area spend about $1,283,348 per year on entertainment admissions).

Based on this market demand, downtown Rutland has seen the development of a new 22,000 SF nine-screen cinemaplex. The viability of renovating the century-old downtown Paramount Theater currently is being assessed.

7. *The Restaurant Niche.* From Portland, ME to Seattle, WA, downtowns have proven to be a conducive environment for the birth and growth of restaurant niches.

The importance of this niche in a downtown revitalization strategy should not be underestimated. Because of the way people behave, this niche can be closely connected to other niches in a very broadly defined "entertainment" niche. For example, people like to go out to dinner before, and sometimes even after, going to a concert, play or movie. And some restaurants, such as the Rainbow Room in New York City, are still "supper clubs" that provide both food and entertainment.

Restaurants can attract diners from trade area residents, tourists and downtown employees. A strong restaurant niche is also an important amenity that can greatly enhance a downtown's ability to attract business tenants, be they corporations or SOHO[37] firms. Furthermore, people have demonstrated a willingness to travel considerable distances to go to a particular restaurant. And popular restaurants such as Peter Luger's, Rao's and Sammy's Romanian in New York City have demonstrated an ability to draw lots of customers despite being located in neighborhoods that display many physical signs of disorder.

While the number of high-quality restaurants in such downtowns as New York, San Francisco, Boston and Chicago have long been well-known, many other downtowns have developed important restaurant "scenes" in recent years. Center City in Philadelphia, for example, now has 19 of the 40 most popular restaurants in the Philadelphia metropolitan area according to a Zagat survey[38] (see Figure 2.5). And within a 1,000-ft. radius of the intersection of South Broad and Walnut — an intersection at the heart of downtown — is a cluster of nine of these most popular restaurants, including those that ranked first, third and fourth.

According to a survey of the readers of *Traveler Magazine*, downtown Philadelphia now has some of the best restaurants in the country, and the restaurants in downtown Cincinnati have long been considered by connoisseurs to be among the nation's finest.

Restaurants have also been keys to such smaller but "hip" downtowns as Santa Monica, CA (for example, Valentino's, Chinois on Main) and Miami Beach, FL (Pacific Time, China Grill). And restaurant niches have grown in what had previously been regarded as very challenging downtown environments. For example, Port Chester, NY for many years had one of the most troubled downtowns in New York State's affluent Westchester County. In recent years, however, it has seen the growth of a niche of more than 20 restaurants. Many of these restaurants were started by Latino and Asian

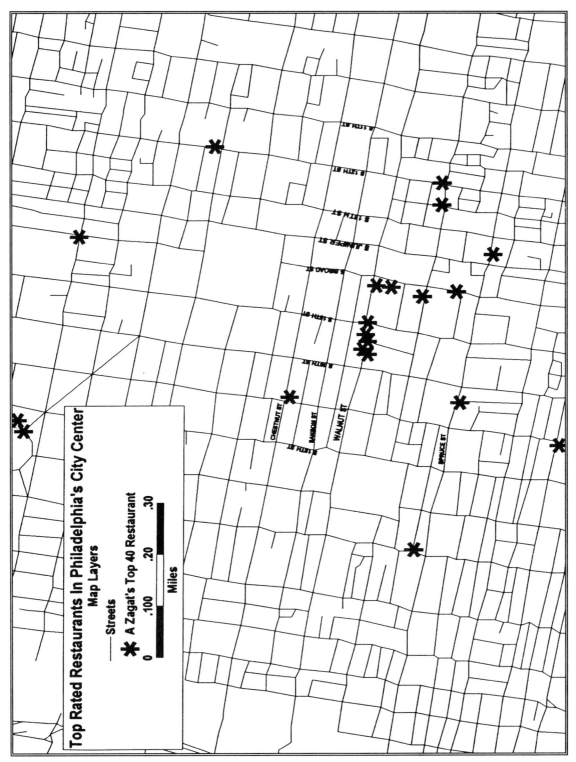

Top Rated Restaurants In Philadelphia's City Center

Map Layers

—— Streets

✳ A Zagat's Top 40 Restaurant

0   .100   .20   .30
Miles

Figure 2.5

immigrants. They were nurtured by comparatively inexpensive rents and nearby Latino and Asian populations. But their success was also an outgrowth of the ability of these entrepreneurs to attract crossover diners from some of America's most upscale residential communities (such as Scarsdale and Rye, NY and Greenwich, CT) which are located nearby.

The Manayunk neighborhood in Philadelphia has only 5,500 residents and a median household income estimated at a modest $31,800.[39] Yet the neighborhood has become one of Philadelphia's trendiest spots. It has combined providing renovated lofts for young, "high-style professionals," with turning its Main Street into a National Historic District. The result has been the emergence of a number of hip shops, galleries and eateries. For example, in 1995, Manayunk had 32 eateries, with 23 being located along its historic Main Street.[40] Two of these restaurants ranked as the seventh and 16th most popular restaurants in Zagat's survey of eateries in the Philadelphia metropolitan region.[41] Some observers feel that the only damper on the growth of this restaurant niche will be the constraints on developing needed additional parking due to the neighborhood's hilly topography and location on a river.

For a number of years, people were not spending as much on eating out as they did during the lofty days of the mid-1980s, but recent data from the Bureau of Labor Statistics indicates that household expenditures in restaurants increased by about two percent between 1992 and 1993. This followed a smaller increase between 1991 and 1992. The Bureau's recent surveys also show that affluent households — those with annual incomes of $70,000 and over — average $4,039 on expenditures for food away from home, while the average household spends just $1,736.[42]

The economic importance of restaurants is demonstrated by a recent market research study for downtown Rutland, VT. The Rutland Partnership's 1994 telephone survey found that the average respondent eats about 58 times a year away from home in a sit-down restaurant. Within Rutland, there was an expenditure potential of $17,277,891 for food and drink away from home, while the sales of such establishments reached over $30 million a year. This indicated that Rutland's eateries sold a lot of meals to tourists or people who lived outside of Rutland. This restaurant "in-shopping" was probably due more to Rutland's economic and government functions that attract shoppers and workers from the trade area than to tourism.

Restaurants are Downtown Rutland's largest retail use, with 35.6 percent of Rutland's 87 establishments being located in this niche.[43] The downtown's eating and drinking establishments occupied about 67,000 SF of retail space and had sales estimated at $10,386,033. Only one restaurant was cited in either the Mobil Travel Guide or the AAA Tourbook (both gave it two stars). But the sheer number of eating and drinking establishments in the downtown and their sales indicated to other restaurant tenant prospects that downtown Rutland was a good place to locate. And indeed, since 1994, a number of better quality eateries have opened. One is a coffee house that was fashioned out of a former bank — the vault is now a private dining room.

Rutland's downtown workers provided a ready lunch-time market worth about $1.6 million to local restaurants, accounting for about 10 percent of the eating and drinking establishments' revenues. Most of these meals were eaten in moderately priced restaurants.

A market study of downtown Upperton, NY found that residents in its Zip Code spent an estimated $29.9 million away from home in eating and drinking establishments in 1993. It is estimated that Upperton's current office workers spent more than $8 million on worktime food and drink in 1995. Together, these statistics represent a total market demand that exceeds $32 million. The 1992 Census of Retail Trade found that restaurants in the Village of Upperton only had sales of $17.35 million. This suggests that there is probably a net exporting of local expenditure dollars amounting to about $14.8 million. The unmet local demand can be used to feed a very sizable expansion of this niche, enabling it to build a physical strength and presence that can attract a large number of additional customers who neither live nor work in Upperton.

The potential for expanding this niche in Upperton is further enhanced by the fact that the existing retail configuration (which has almost 500,000 SF of department store space, including Saks, Lord & Taylor and Sears) attracts shoppers from 138,574 households, who visit the area at least once a month. These shoppers eat meals at restaurants more than 9.3 million times a year. Upperton's restaurants could capture many more of these dining dollars.

Within the primary upscale trade area of downtown White Plains, NY, survey results indicate that residents dine in sit-down restaurants about 1,042,000 times a year, and, in 1993, they spent about $236,133,000 on eating and drinking away from home. It is estimated that office workers in downtown White Plains potentially spent as much as $7.5 million in downtown restaurants and bars — this would be equivalent to about 41 percent of the revenues of such establishments that year. This shows that office workers can have a very significant impact on the restaurant niche.[44]

8. *The Arts.* In 1991, the performing arts nationally had $4.7 billion in admission receipts, compared to $4.8 billion for spectator sports events and $3.7 billion for motion picture theaters.[45] In many communities, attendance at cultural events exceeds attendance at sporting events: For example, in 1992-93, about 5,817,000 people attended the games of the Denver Nuggets, Denver Broncos and Colorado Rockies in Denver, CO, while 7,299,000 people attended cultural events in the city.[46]

A study conducted in 1992 found that 59 percent of the visitors to arts institutions in the 17-county New York-New Jersey metropolitan region came from outside of the region — meaning, they could be considered tourists.[47] Moreover, almost 50 percent of these "tourists" reported that the main purpose of their trip was to attend cultural activities.[48] The estimated economic effect of these "arts-motivated visitors" in 1992 on New York City was very significant, with their expenditures supporting 32,132 jobs and having a total impact of adding $2.45 billion to the city's economy.[49]

Many downtowns across the country have learned how to use the arts both to provide amenities to downtown visitors and to stimulate further revitalization.

Downtown Concerts. Many, many downtowns operate concert series, either outdoors or inside downtown churches, auditoriums, museums, concert halls or office building lobbies. In 1995, Collierville, TN (population 23,000) ran a series of nine free summer concerts on Thursday evenings that attracted an average audience of 450 people. The Buffalo Place downtown district runs a similar evening series, "Thursday on the Square," that averages about 5,000 attendees for each concert.[50]

Many other downtowns operate noontime concert series for the benefit of office workers and shoppers.

Major Cultural Institutions. A number of major downtowns have created performing arts centers. Two of the most famous are Lincoln Center in New York City and the John F. Kennedy Center for the Performing Arts in Washington, D.C. But in downtown Newark, NJ, an area which has suffered from riots, high crime and the flight of over half of its population, construction is nearing completion on a $180-million performing arts center that is intended both to be the cornerstone of its future revitalization and to position downtown Newark as a major national player in the arts. Located on a 12-acre site, this project will contain a 2,750-seat theater and concert hall, a

500-seat theater and comparable rehearsal space. Plans are already set for a New Jersey World Festival which will feature in its first year the culture of the Portuguese, who constitute one of the largest ethnic groups in Newark.[51]

One of the most interesting stories about how major cultural institutions can drive downtown revitalization is that of Lincoln Road in Miami Beach, FL.[52] This once-fashionable Art Deco pedestrian mall had fallen on hard times by the late 1970s as the South Beach area in which it was located went into significant decline. By the mid-1980s, the cost of space along Lincoln Road had lowered to the point that it was very affordable for fledgling cultural groups. The New World Symphony took one of the vacant Art Deco theaters and renovated it into a performance space for famed ballet director Edward Vilella. An old department store was refurbished for a practice hall[53] and administrative offices for the Miami City Ballet. Then, in 1984, the South Florida Arts Center opened.

Over the intervening years, art galleries, fashionable restaurants and specialty retail shops were attracted to the Art Deco, artistic ambiance of the mall, and they added their own "funky" character that enhanced the mall's charm. Now — as South Beach has become a major location for shooting photographs for advertising agencies and an increasingly important place for making movies and doing TV and recordings for the Latino and Latin American markets — the Lincoln Road Mall is attracting major entertainment tenants such as MTV Latino and Sony Music International. Major national retail chains are reportedly also showing interest.

Another interesting case is Santa Cruz, CA, a coastal university town with a population of about 49,000. It has plans to develop a full downtown block into a multifunctional performing arts center that will contain a rehabilitated 720-seat theater, a 250-seat studio theater converted from a former bank building and a newly constructed 1,200-seat concert hall.[54]

Because of its location, this performing arts facility will be able to be "embraced (by) restaurants, cafes, coffee houses, movie screens, night clubs...."[55]

Another key project in downtown Santa Cruz's broad entertainment niche, a nine-screen cinemaplex, opened in May 1995.

In Rockford, IL, a consortium of six very diverse visual and performing arts institutions has promoted the development and programs of the new

Riverfront Museum Park. The heart of this project is a 120,000-SF museum that was formerly a Sears, Roebuck store. This project thrusted the downtown forward as its region's arts center.[56]

When their downtown suffered from the arrival of 900-lb. retail gorillas on its periphery, community leaders in Mt. Airy, NC, created the Mount Airy Museum of Regional History, a visitors center and a downtown crafts market.[57]

The strength of the John Harms Center for the Performing Arts in downtown Englewood, NJ, demonstrates how strong an attraction the arts can be even for a community of just 26,000 people located less than 30 minutes from New York's Lincoln Center and the famous theaters along Broadway. According to one high-level executive, last year the Center attracted over 180,000 patrons in an eight-month season.

Crafts. The level of national consumer interest in crafts should not be underestimated. A very large national survey conducted in 1992 by the U.S. Bureau of the Census for the National Endowment for the Arts found that 54 percent of the respondents had attended an arts/crafts fair in the past year.[58]

In general, it may be a good idea for downtowns to focus on craftsmen-produced houseware items such as furniture, rugs, textiles, ceramics and glassware, etc., though they must be of very high quality if they are to succeed in upscale markets. Such craftsmen can help make a downtown's furniture/home furnishings niche unique within its trade area. Moreover, having craftsmen not only selling their wares, but visible to the public as they make them, can add a performance quality to the retail setting. This is done in the Torpedo Factory in Alexandria, VA, and in Simon Pearce's mill project in Quechee, VT.

Crafts can also be a good way for downtowns to attract upscale shoppers. For example, the trade area telephone survey performed for downtown White Plains found that for households in the $75,000 to $100,000 and $100,000-plus income categories, going to crafts shops and galleries was their second most frequent arts-related activity with an average of 4.12 and 4.22 visits per year, respectively.[59]

9. *Downtown "Entertainment-Based" Retail Centers.* In the 1980s, a number of downtowns seemed to become instantaneously revitalized when what were to become known as Festival Markets opened up. A concept developed

and made famous by the Rouse Company in such projects as Faneuil Hall and Adams Market in Boston, Harborside in Baltimore and the South Street Seaport in Lower Manhattan, these centers focused on projecting and marketing a unique recreational atmosphere that clearly differentiated them from traditional department store or chain store retailing. Research by the Downtown Research & Development Center found that in four of these centers on which data was compiled, that restaurants, fast food operations and food markets accounted for between 42 percent and 62 percent of their GLA.[60] The food combined with street performers and festive banners give the centers a definite entertainment-oriented ambiance. It is to enjoy this ambiance, more than to purchase any type of goods or service, that motivates throngs of people to visit these markets.

These markets are also powerful attractions for out-of-town visitors. Between 25 to 45 percent of their shoppers can be tourists.[61]

Urban Entertainment Centers.[62] In recent years, major downtown retail projects have emerged that are even more overtly entertainment-oriented. One of the best examples of this trend is Cocowalk in the heart of the Coconut Grove neighborhood in Miami, FL. This neighborhood — Miami's Greenwich Village — has long been known for its artistic community and its downtown has had a strong emphasis on entertainment-type establishments. Cocowalk has a GLA of 157,140 SF, of which about 60 percent is devoted to such entertainment-related uses as restaurants, nightclubs and a 16-screen movie theater.[63] The center has the reputation of being one of the "hottest spots" in the Miami area. It has over three million visitors a year, a large proportion of whom are tourists. In 1992, sales averaged a very impressive $480/SF. The synergy between elements of the center is obvious to the interested observer.

Dallas Alley is located in the West End Historic District of downtown Dallas, TX. It is a collection of clubs, dining rooms and arcade amusements that is located in a former Sunshine Biscuit Company building that has gross sales of $8.3 million.[64] Dallas Alley fits in well with the West End Marketplace Cinema and Planet Hollywood and together they have created a critical mass and made the Historic District the number one reason for people to come downtown.

10. *Value Retailing Niche.* Stores in this niche can be "category killers" or "big box retailers," large discounters or manufacturers' outlets. The category killers can occupy between 30,000 SF and 120,000 SF and tend to specialize

in specific kinds of merchandise — for example, Toys 'R' Us and CompUSA. Large discounters, such as Wal-Mart and Costco, offer a wider array of merchandise, though at distinctly low prices. Their space requirements are normally in the 50,000 SF to 120,000 SF range. A factory outlet is a store owned and operated by a manufacturer, which sells its brands of merchandise in the store at prices that are 30 to 75 percent below those in department stores. An individual manufacturer's outlet may only occupy between 1,500 and 2,000 SF, but they often are clustered together in outlet centers that can have over 200,000 SF of selling space. Outlet sales average about $243/SF annually.[65]

Surprisingly, while value retailing is definitely popular, it is not always the type of shopping that consumers are requesting the most. For example, the survey of White Plains' trade area residents found that 14.3 percent would like to see more discount stores and factory outlets opened downtown, but 23.5 percent wanted more boutiques and high-quality specialty shops.[66]

For many communities, large value retailers are the very 900-lb. retail gorillas that downtown merchants fear and try to keep out of their market areas. But in a growing number of communities, downtown leaders are vigorously trying to develop a value retail niche and they are actively recruiting chains such as Wal-Mart, Bradlees, CompUSA, Borders Books and Music, Linens 'n' Things and Staples. Other downtowns have attracted factory outlet centers.

Big Boxes Downtown. While suburban markets are saturated with retail options, urban markets are relatively under-served and consequently "represent the next horizon in retail growth potential."[67]

A project in the Fenway neighborhood of Boston demonstrates this trend. A former Sears warehouse distribution center is being turned into a four-story, 560,000 SF category-killer retail mall. The average store will occupy 40,000 SF. Among the tenants are a 65,000 SF supermarket and a sporting goods store.[68]

In Waltham, MA, Gateway Plaza, a 130,000 SF retail project, is spearheading the downtown's revitalization. The anchor tenant in this project is a 105,000 SF Bradlees.[69]

In North Boulder, CO, a new village center is being constructed around a project that will have a 55,000-SF supermarket, 48,000 SF of ancillary retail space, 23,000 SF of office space, 67 residential units, a 4,000-SF daycare facility and an 8,800-SF library.[70]

In downtown Rutland, VT, Wal-Mart is opening a 76,000-SF store in the Rutland Plaza Shopping Center. This location was previously occupied by a Kmart that has since moved to a newly constructed nearby regional mall. Also in Rutland Plaza are a 28,000-SF T.J. Maxx and a 58,000-SF Price Chopper supermarket. The Rutland Partnership, the downtown's management organization, warmly welcomed Wal-Mart. According to Dick Courcelle, the Partnership's executive director:

> "A large value retailer like Wal-Mart significantly expands a downtown's trade area. With Wal-Mart, more people will shop downtown more often, from morning until night, seven days a week. With a larger consumer base generated by a retail giant, there are greater opportunities for multi-purpose visits with other downtown specialty retail stores, services and restaurants. Having Wal-Mart in the heart of our downtown is a win-win situation for us."[71]

The State of Vermont has made a concerted effort to have Wal-Mart locate their stores in downtowns. As one state official said, "We were very vehement that Wal-Mart does not belong in sprawl locations."[72]

Stamford, CT, is another downtown that is trying to develop this niche. As the executive director of its downtown district stated: "We are not opposed to big box retailing: We are the chief proponents of it."[73]

Downtown Factory Outlet Centers. One of the attractions of downtown locations for this niche is the existence of large, attractive old buildings that can be put to a retail use at a reasonable cost. As one expert states: "The charm of these older buildings, with their sense of history and tradition, are an attraction for many factory outlet chains because their upscale customers enjoy such ambiance."[74]

Some communities with downtown outlets are:

• Stroud, OK, where a Tangier Outlet Mall opened in 1992 and resulted in a doubling of downtown retail sales, increased customer traffic, a general improvement in the downtown's appearance and higher property values.[75]

• Durango, CO, where old storefronts were combined with new construction to develop an outlet center on the edge of the downtown.

- Chattanooga, TN, where former railroad warehouses in the downtown area have been turned into an outlet mall that has continued to expand.

- Lake Placid, NY, which has a 20,000-SF outlet center.

- Flemington, NJ, which also has a significant downtown outlet center.

Because outlet centers have a unique set of location requirements, such as their proximity to large malls and department stores, they are not appropriate for every downtown.

Office and High-Tech Niches

During the 1980s, office development provided the economic engine for the revitalization of many downtowns. Major regional banks and utilities were often headquartered downtown and their "back office" operations required large amounts of downtown office space. For example, it was the growth of NCNB (now Nationsbank), First Union and Wachovia banks and their office workers that drove the revitalization of the central business district in Charlotte, NC. Although the nature of the office space market has changed significantly,[76] downtowns continue to have vital and unique assets that underpin their attractiveness as business locations, often for firms on the leading edge of their fields.

1. *County Seat Functions.* The strongest assets of many downtowns are derived from their historical development as county seats, and those downtowns with these assets will not soon lose them. County seats typically have county, municipal and perhaps state and federal offices. They are joined invariably by various courts and sometimes by independent agencies. Large county seats are usually also regional financial centers, with many banks, brokerage and real estate firms. And they are often the sites of large hospitals. Because doctors and lawyers like to be near the hospitals and courts in which they frequently must work, county seats also usually attract many lawyers' and doctors' offices. These professionals are often joined by accountants, auditors and management consultants who are drawn by the government agencies, financial firms and the rest of the professional community.

Downtown White Plains, NY, for example, captures a majority share of the city's firms in the two industries in which its county seat functions appear to particularly assert themselves: It has 61 percent of the city's legal services firms and 66.7 percent of those dealing with title abstracts. It also has fairly strong shares of the city's commercial banks (42.2%), mortgage bankers (47.6%) and security brokers and dealers (42.9%). Since White Plains as a whole has about 37 percent of all the legal services firms in its county and about 52 percent of that industry's employees, it appears that the downtown also has a very important share of the county's legal services firms.

Downtowns across the country have also found that, while they lost the large office installations of major corporations such as IBM, NYNEX and AT&T due to mergers, downsizing, cost-cutting and corporate re-engineering, they were far less likely to lose firms whose activities related to their county seat functions.

2. *Research Complexes*. Downtowns often are the homes of large hospitals and universities. These can be the anchors of substantial research and development as well as high technology production centers. Such centers can bring thousands of new jobs downtown. They can also help the downtown project an image of a business location that is prepared for the 21st century.

Downtown locations close to a major research hospital or university are often quite attractive to high-tech companies because they provide easy access to major research facilities, their libraries and, most importantly, their skilled personnel. The first-rate scientists at these downtown institutions are extremely busy and do not want to travel far to interface with their related business interests, even if they are owners. Small high-tech firms also do not do well in rural settings, which will lack the required support services that can range from printers and copy centers to research libraries, translators and distributors of special scientific equipment.

An example of a potential research complex niche is the Virginia Biotechnology Research Park which is being developed as a joint venture by Virginia Commonwealth University, the City of Richmond, the Commonwealth of Virginia and the business community. When completed, it is expected to add 3,000 new jobs on 20 acres of vacant land in downtown Richmond. The 1.5 million SF research and development complex will represent a capital investment of $180 million. The center is across the street from the Medical College of Virginia, whose facility has one of the strongest life science research programs in the nation.

In 1989, the Downtown Development District in New Orleans created a medical task force to work with private businesses, the city and the State of Louisiana to determine how the downtown could benefit from the growth potential of the city's health care industry. The result was the creation of the New Orleans Regional Medical Center (NORMC), which brings together four major institutions: the Medical Center of Louisiana, the Tulane University Medical Center, the Louisiana State University Medical Center and the Veterans Administration Medical Center. By the year 2000, the center will occupy a 35-block area of the downtown, add over 8,200 new jobs and have an economic impact of approximately $1.9 billion in investments.

The potential economic impact of hospitals can be demonstrated by the Moses Campus of the Montefiore Medical Center in Norwood, a mature urban neighborhood of about 42,000 residents in the north-central part of the Bronx, NY. In 1992, the area had over 270,000 SF of office space, with a vacancy rate of 11 percent, a comparatively low rate for the region. The medical center leased about 75,000 SF of off-campus space, and in previous years had generated a demand for about 30,000 SF of additional space annually. In addition, the offices of 121 doctors, 43 dentists and four medical laboratories were located within a one-half mile radius of the medical center.

Small high-tech firms have also demonstrated a desire to be close to other, similar firms. As one observer has noted, such propinquity generates opportunities "for chance encounters, where my two cents and your two cents equals eight cents or 10 cents."[77] In Lower Manhattan, Rudin Management, a building owner, working closely with the Alliance for Downtown New York, is trying to develop a number of older buildings, with comparatively small floor plates, into an "interactive technology enclave." The first building in this venture is reportedly leasing out at a brisk rate. It has been renovated to provide the type of "wiring" that small, high-tech firms require, such as enhanced electric power, satellite uplinks and four types of telecommunications systems. But the owners have found that "community is the most important thing we are selling here."[78] Many of the tenants like running into each other in the hallways and elevators. They congregate in the lobby. They knock on each other's doors with ideas. And they often use each other's services. The Alliance is also trying to foster this sense of community by attracting restaurants and art galleries and by converting other office buildings into 1,000 residential units. It is hoped that "many of the residential tenants will be in the information technology business, people who want to create a seamlessness between home and work life."[79]

Modern communication technology can also give a development boost to smaller downtowns. In Winchester, VA, for example, the General Services Administration turned an old downtown building into a modern telecommuting center for federal workers. Such centers appeal to office workers who spend a lot of time traveling to work, or people who find working at home too distracting.[80]

As Figure 2.6 indicates, downtowns can be great locations for small businesses, especially new ones in high-tech industries. Older downtown buildings can provide the comparatively small amounts of affordable and reasonably attractive office space that many small firms require. In a downtown, a small business owner or office worker can easily walk to a broad profusion of services such as banks, lawyers, accountants, government

Some Potential Downtown Advantages As A Location For Small Businesses
- The presence of "expert" product users
- A nearby university or college to provide supplementary management and technical expertise
- Comparatively inexpensive space costs
- A charming and active local environment
- An environment that facilitates "networking"
    — technological
    — human
    — financial
- Nests for "Lone Eagles"

Figure 2.6

offices and archives, travel agents, employment agencies, printers, computer shops, libraries and book stores. Also, in a downtown the small business owner may have a number of customers or potential customers. Downtowns also can provide new entrepreneurs easy opportunities to network with other businesspersons, which can lead to the transfer of technological information and the identification of new customer prospects — as the situation in Lower Manhattan described above amply demonstrates. An often overlooked downtown advantage is that the many companies, government offices and hospitals located in downtown can provide small firms with "expert users" who can be vital when small firms are developing new products. For example, courts can be helpful in the development of court calendaring programs as hospitals can be in the development of medical instruments. Finally, downtown universities and hospitals also can provide small firms with a large, local pool of skilled workers.

CHAPTER 3
MAJOR NATIONAL AND REGIONAL TRENDS

Overview

One of the first steps in developing a niche strategy for your downtown is to ascertain the strength and direction of major national and regional trends. These trends, over which local leaders can exercise little control, will shape the opportunities of local property owners and business operators to survive and grow. These forces will also have an impact on the types of retailers and office tenants that might be interested in locating in your downtown. Consequently, any revitalization strategy being prepared for your downtown must take these forces into account. The discussion below is meant to be illustrative and identifies some of the trends that have been affecting many downtowns.

The Aging of the Baby Boomers

Toward the end of the recent recession, experts began to realize that retail sales had been falling off since about 1987, and therefore reflected the impacts of a number of long-term forces, rather than the short-term cyclical factors typically associated with a recession.

Among the most important of these new trends is the aging and indebtedness of the "baby boomers." The baby boomers constitute a huge bulge in our population and include people born from 1946 through the late 1950s. As the baby boomers age during the 1990s, the number of Americans entering the 45- to 54-year-old age group will increase at an annual rate of 3.9 percent, while the number of Americans entering the 25- to 34-year-old age group will decline at an annual rate of 1.7 percent.

The baby boomers have had a huge effect on the nation's retailing and overall economy. During their 20s and 30s, they formed households and created a large demand for housing and household goods and furnishings. As they had children, boomers bought them clothing, shoes, radios, televisions, etc. As their careers were still before them, the boomers were optimistic about the future and built up their debt levels by buying homes and consumer goods.

In contrast, Americans over age 40 have traditionally spent less and saved more: Their households are furnished, their careers have plateaued, their children are grown and they face the prospect of retirement. Thus, we can expect baby boomers to spend much less on retail goods over the coming years. At the same time there will be fewer and fewer people in the younger age brackets — demographic groups that have an historically higher propensity to spend money on retail goods.

The baby boomers had a habit of "trading up," of not just buying possessions, but of buying better and better possessions than their parents had. Instead of buying a pair of $35 Levi's, they would purchase $80 designer jeans; instead of a Huffy bike they would buy a Peugeot. They tended to ignore bargain basements, but frequented *chic* boutiques.

But, as the baby boomers aged, they began to "downscale." As one expert described it:

"People are...buying Oneida stainless-steel silverware instead of European stainless and sterling. Forty-five-inch projection televisions are out. Rental video tapes are in. Fleece is in. Italian suits are out. Levi's are in. People are buying a Huffy bike instead of a Peugeot."[81]

Baby boomers are now looking for more moderately priced goods and to appreciate good values. They are the main market supporting the niche that has come to be called "value retailing," which includes "off-price" retailers, manufacturers outlets and mass retailers who rely on everyday low prices, such as Wal-Mart, Kmart, Target, Costco Price, Waban, Home Depot, T.J. Maxx, etc. By 1993, "value retailers" had captured about 44 percent of the market for department store-type merchandise, otherwise known as GAFO or "comparison shoppers goods."[82]

Some downtowns, such as those in White Plains, NY, New Rochelle, NY, Rutland, VT and Brooklyn, NY or neighborhood "Main Streets" like Fordham Road in the Bronx, have been able to attract some of these value retailers. Many others have not and, consequently, have lost additional market share.

Affluent Households

Households with incomes over $75,000 have much greater discretionary spending power than average and are not impacted in quite the same way as baby boomers with lower incomes. For example, a 1993 national study of affluent households found that:

> "Among those in households earning $75,000 and over, clothing purchases last year were considerably above average. For affluent women, it would appear that practicality dominated. Raincoats or all-weather coats, business-type suits and business dress pants were additions to the wardrobe. The party, even in pinched times, does seem to go on with purchasing of cocktail or formal dresses 35 percent above average among this segment."[83]

The same study found that "early baby boomers," those between the ages of 35 and 44 and just entering early middle age, represent a disproportionately strong market for firms offering "home remodeling and improvement products and services."[84] They also are in the vanguard of computer ownership and usage.[85] Affluent "empty nesters" have very high travel rates, to both domestic and foreign destinations.[86]

Tapping this affluent market has been the key to the success of Rodeo Drive in Beverly Hills, CA. The emergence of New York City's Madison Avenue between 57th and 72nd Streets as the hottest shopping area in Manhattan is also based on its ability to serve very affluent shoppers. Ridgewood, NJ, Greenwich, CT, Westport, CT and Rye, NY are some small downtowns in the NY-NJ-CT metropolitan region that have successfully attracted wealthy shoppers from nearby residential areas.

The 'Baby Boomlet'

While a good deal of the population is entering middle age, there has been a surge in births nationally — some call it the "baby boomlet" — with over four million babies being born every year since 1989. As an article in *The New York Times* so vividly described it: "If the baby boom is a pig passing through a python, the python has taken another gulp."[87] This new bulge in demand has already shown its strength in the recent strong increase in the demand for multimedia personal computers. It should also manifest itself in such markets as children's clothing, toys and furniture and shift to other goods and services as this population bulge matures.

Age Structure Changes

The aging of the baby boomers nationally means that most local market areas that are not attracting a lot of new immigrants, be they foreign or domestic, will have an aging population. Within the 31-county New York City metropolitan area, for example, an important swing in the population's age will occur by the year 2005. According to the Regional Plan Association's projections, between 1985 and 2005, the region will gain about 3.5 million people over 35 years of age and will have 1.5 million fewer people under 35.[88] This change in the region's age structure will have great impacts on the demand for medical services, housing and retail goods.

The Growth in the Minority/Ethnic Population

As was mentioned in Chapter 2 (page 7), ethnic minorities account for about 70 percent of U.S. population growth, and, by the year 2020, they will account for about 65 percent of the nation's total population. The impact of this growth will be enormous in many parts of the United States. For example, in the 31-county New York City metropolitan region, the Regional Plan Association (see Figure 3.1) forecasts that this population segment, which increased its share of the

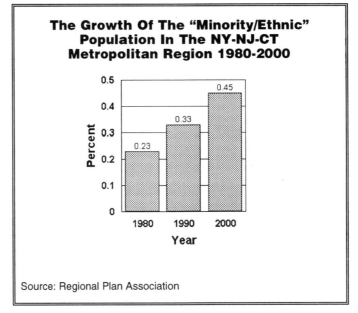

Figure 3.1

region's total population from 23 percent in 1980 to 33 percent in 1990, will increase its share to 45 percent by 2000.[89] This population segment's growth is the result of both immigration and higher birth rates.

These ethnic markets are now supporting a significant number of downtown retail areas such as those mentioned in Chapter II: Fulton Mall in downtown Brooklyn, Main Street in Flushing, NY and Bergenline Avenue in West New York, NJ.

Fewer Shopping Trips

During the late 1970s and early 1980s, it appeared that shopping had taken on the function of being a major recreational activity in the United States. Suburban malls began to perform the social functions of our older downtowns — people went to malls not only because they needed to buy some goods or services, but also to stroll and meet friends and neighbors. Mall shopping became a national pastime that far surpassed baseball.

But toward the close of the 1980s, evidence suggests that Americans began to shop less frequently, visit fewer stores on each shopping trip and spend less time shopping at the mall each month. During this decade, the average number of mall trips per month fell from 3.1 to 2. The amount of time spent at malls fell even more significantly from 12 to 4 hours a month, and the number of stores visited was halved (7 to 3.5).[90]

The reasons for this new trend are uncertain. Some potential explanations are:

- Malls, having saturated the nation, no longer provide a novel experience.

- The baby boomers have aged and have less money for shopping.

- With more and more two career households, people have less time for shopping, especially "recreational shopping."

Telephone surveys in New Jersey and Vermont have shown that, with the exception of retired people, the trend toward household members having less time for shopping is very strong. Time-stressed shoppers are especially likely to appreciate a wide selection of immediately available merchandise and goods and services. They also are likely to prefer shopping closer to home, if they can get the appropriate service and merchandise.

Downtowns Have Become More Attractive to Developers and Retail Chains

For some time now, real estate developers have been facing the fact that appropriate "greenfield" sites for constructing traditional malls are harder and harder to find. They now are looking at highly urbanized locations that they rejected in the past. And they are developing types of shopping centers that are quite different from the traditional malls, such as fashion centers, anchorless specialty centers and urban vertical malls. In Chicago, for example, developers are planning a 400,000-SF mall geared, in design and store mix, to Hispanic shoppers.[91]

This strategy is also being followed by more and more retail chains, a propensity which has been reinforced by the recent financial weaknesses of major department store chains, the traditional anchors of suburban malls. Also, as a recent article in *Women's Wear Daily* headlined, "Malls' Malaise Leads to a Revival for Main Street USA,"[92] chains also have discovered that pedestrian traffic can be more important than auto traffic as an indicator of store sales. So, it is no longer surprising to find:

- a Gap on 34th Street in Manhattan, on Steinway Street in Astoria, NY, in downtown New Haven, CT and downtown Ridgewood, NJ

- a Toys 'R' Us, Nobody Beats the Wiz and Barnes & Noble in downtown Brooklyn

- a Starbucks or Coffee Connection in downtown Mt. Kisco, NY, downtown Englewood, NJ and Great Neck Plaza, NY

- an Ann Taylor in downtown Ridgewood and downtown Englewood

- a Kmart and Price Club opening on 34th Street in Manhattan

Many of these chains have become fully aware of the conditions usually found in downtowns, and apparently they are increasingly finding acceptable ways of dealing with them. Their complaints about downtowns are more and more about the nature of the available space and less about the market opportunities a downtown location can provide. Indeed, many chains realize that downtown locations allow them to target previously untapped markets.[93]

But these chains are not rushing into just any downtown or village square. They are looking for areas that have a proven level of customer traffic. None want to be a "pioneer" or the anchor that the other on-street shops can live off of. Also, they want trade areas whose residents mesh with their customer profiles as well as attractive downtown streetscapes and store facades.

The obvious, but very significant, implication of this trend is that downtowns capable of providing a safe, attractive environment can now begin to develop niches that would have been unthinkable just five years ago.

There Has Been a Structural Change in the Office Market

Recent trends indicate a structural change has occurred in the nature of the demand for office space:

- Downsizing has reduced the number of middle managers and technicians.

- Mergers have enabled greater efficiency with fewer workers and less office space.

- More corporate employees are telecommuting.[94]

- Increasingly, large corporations are using such techniques as "hoteling," where salesmen and service providers (such as accountants) who spend most of their time in the field will share office space. Some major companies that "hotel" office space are IBM, AT&T, Price Waterhouse and Travelers Insurance.

Because of telecommunications improvements, lower space and labor costs and higher worker productivity, more major corporations in the NY-NJ-CT metropolitan region are placing headquarters and large back office operations in locations outside of the region. For example, Salomon Brothers moved 800 employees to Tampa, FL; Morgan Stanley has backup computer operations in Delaware; Mobil moved their headquarters to Virginia; and NatWest moved theirs to Scranton, PA.

- Corporations have reduced the amount of space provided for each worker from an average of about 250 SF in the 1980s to about 175 SF today.

- Corporations looking for space are less interested in prestigious addresses and more in costs. More than ever, the cost of space is the number one criteria corporations use in evaluating potential new office locations.

- Many of the corporations now looking for space are looking for cheaper space than they now have.

- Other growing location criteria are the quality of life to be found both in the commercial area and the surrounding residential neighborhoods and the presence of a nearby commuter rail station.

The Small Office/Home Office Market

The growth of new home-based micro-businesses has been phenomenal since the PC became generally available and corporations adopted "outsourcing" strategies. While many of these new businesses are apt to maintain their "micro" stature and be home-based, many others are looking for office space because of their need for a more sociable work environment, the interference of children or spouses, etc. Such start-ups may be good tenant prospects for some vacant downtown office space.

The importance of these firms should not be underestimated. A recent report on California's economy found that it had rebounded from a devastating recession during the early 1990s, creating more than 500,000 new jobs to replace those lost in the aerospace, defense and other traditional industries. Most of these new jobs have been in the growth-oriented computer software, biotechnology, multimedia and entertainment industries.[95]

These growth industries tend to be composed of networks of small, specialized firms and research institutions. And these firms tend to operate like those in Hollywood and film production, industries characterized by networks of flexible, temporary or virtual organizations and freelance professionals brought together for specific projects.[96]

Philip M. Burgess, the president of the Center for the New West, has coined the term "lone eagles" to denote those who are able to live far from their job sites because of their use of computers, modems, fax machines and telephones. Others refer to this group as "open-collar workers."[97] While some of the lone eagles are still on corporate payrolls (for example, many of those being hoteled), others are independent consultants, advisors and other professionals who sell their services to a variety of clients. Some also start firms that have more than one employee. Many of these freelancers are the "victims of down-sizing, relayering and other forms of corporate re-engineering." Burgess estimates that as many as one-third of the corporate staff and middle managers laid off during the last recession were hired by their former employers as "outsourcers."[98]

Another defining feature of lone eagles is their concern for good quality of life, exploiting their utilization of computers and sophisticated communications devices to allow them to move to any geographic area that has the kind of living conditions they are looking for. It is precisely this concern about quality-of-life issues that many suburban downtowns can use to help assure their economic future.

Following Burgess' analysis, one might expect that the same corporate "re-engineering" that led IBM, AT&T and other major corporations to return so much prime office space to the market, also generated a very large pool of lone eagles. Many of them already live in neighborhoods with satisfactory quality-of-life attributes that are within a 10- to 15-minute drive of a downtown. Among them is a subgroup that will need suitable office space or a telework facility. They may find the nearby downtown a very attractive office location. This is the office niche of the future for many small and medium-sized suburban and rural downtowns.

CHAPTER 4
HOW TO FIND NICHES AND ASSESS THEIR VIABILITY

Finding Your Downtown's Niches

There are a number of steps that a downtown organization should take in performing this vital function. Some can be done by its staff members since they involve the use of very basic information that a downtown organization should be gathering as part of its standard operating procedures. The analysis of such data may require some imagination, but not any sophisticated technical knowledge. Other methods of identifying downtown niches, however, do require sophisticated research skills and may require outside assistance. The discussion below is meant to provide a downtown organization with some of the basic information it will need:

- if it decides to use its staff to identify its downtown's niches; or

- to write useful Requests For Proposals and evaluate consultants it might hire to carry out this task.

1. *Identifying Existing Niches.* Existing niches are a boon for downtowns because they do not have to be created — they just have to become organized. Consequently, they provide a downtown organization with a key building block on which to grow by:

- enlarging each existing niche through recruiting more businesses; and

- advertising and promoting the niche to bring more shoppers and visitors downtown.

Strangely, many downtowns have existing niches that are totally unrecognized. For example, no one was aware of downtown Rutland, VT's "wedding niche" or downtown Englewood, NJ's "home center niche" until an intentional effort was made to identify niches. So, one of the first things that a downtown organization should do is search for its commercial district's existing niches:

Look at Niches in Comparable Downtowns. Niches that are successful in comparable downtowns are often a good indication of what to look for in your own business center. For example, the possibility of an unnoticed wedding niche in downtown Rutland was caught by an observer who had just visited downtown White Plains, NY and was intrigued by the cluster of bridal shops there.

Take Long Walks. Downtown district managers often walk through their domain as part of their everyday duties. Coincidentally, one of the best ways of identifying existing niches is by pounding the pavement on foot and looking closely at the types of business operations that are present in your downtown. Do not expect just one pass through your downtown to be productive: sometimes it may take a number of pass-throughs over a three- or even a six-month time period. But, there is no better way for identifying existing niches than walking your downtown!

Look at Photographs and/or Slides. This is a good adjunct method to walking the downtown. It often is very time efficient. Photos and slides are also the best way of demonstrating to others the existing downtown niches that have been found. And, they can be used for marketing and promotional purposes.

Analyze Your Downtown Commercial Space Inventory. An effective downtown organization usually has a reliable database containing information about the commercial space in its district. Such a database should not only contain information about ownership, square footage and tenancy, but also facts about economic function, perhaps using the Census Bureau's Standard Industrial Code, or SIC. SIC numbers are useful in identifying existing downtown niches (see Table 4.1).

Obtain and Analyze Sales Data. The Census of Retail Trades provides sales data for many downtowns broken down by SIC numbers. Private firms specializing in producing market research data can often provide Zip Code-level estimates of retail sales, usually broken down by two-digit SIC codes: These are usually manipulations of Census Bureau data that provide "updated" figures.

Obtain and Analyze Listings of Firms in Your District from Sources on CD-ROM. Market research firms such as American Business Information, Select

Sample Inventory Of A Downtown's Commercial Space

No.	Street	Occupant	Owner/Taxpayer	SIC	Street Level Com'l Space
Misc Manufacturing/Jewelry Precious Metals					**900**
951	Commerce	Jewels By Remarqu	Mr. Ed Muller	391100	900
Transportation by Air					**2,950**
1001	Commerce	Federal Express	The Upperton Company	451202	2,950
Transportation Services					**975**
945	Commerce	Take Off Travel	Mr. Ed Muller	472400	975
Retail					**124,200**
910	Commerce	Pay Day	Upperton,Inc. c/o AtoZ Stores Inc.	531100	60,000
880	Commerce	Mary's Bridal Shop	Revland Realty	562101	2,400
953	Commerce	Bonny's Formal & Bridal		562101	2,000
937	Commerce	Aristocrat Furs	Colbin Development	563201	1,200
1046	Commerce	Furs By Barbara	Upperton Associates	563201	2,500
870	Commerce	Formal Shoes	Revlane Realty	566101	1,600
976	Commerce	Ed Mitchell Tailors	The Upperton Company	569904	1,425
994	Commerce	Melbeyan Carpets	The Upperton Company	571300	1,425
840	Commerce	Franks	FrankUpperton Realty	571905	15,600
825	Commerce	Edmundo's Restaurant		581299	3,500
874	Commerce	Allegria Restaurant	RevlanD Realty	581299	2,500
919	Commerce	Brass Lily Restaurant	Colbin Development	581299	1,520
931	Commerce	Upper Crust Cafe Restaurant	Colbin Development	581299	1,200
980	Commerce	From The Vine Restaurant	The Upperton Company	581299	2,280
820	Commerce	CVS Drug Store	Frank Upperton Realty	591205	10,000
990	Commerce	Lazeri Rugs	The Upperton Company	593201	3,895
949	Commerce	Book Store	Mr. Ed Muller,	594200	2,175
815	Commerce	Net Jewlers	Jerome Hoffman	594499	2,880
827	Commerce	Pluto Photo	Jerome Hoffman	594600	4,500
923	Commerce	Upperton Galleries	Colbin Development	599969	1,600
F.I.R.E. Industries					**14,950**
975	Commerce	Dime Savings Bank	Franklin Enterprises	602200	9,600
935	Commerce	Charles Schwab	Colbin Development	621101	2,400
1001	Commerce	Merrill Lynch	The Upperton Company	621101	2,950
Personal & Business Services					**4,625**
1042	Commerce	Jenny Craig	Upperton Associates	729901	3,200
984	Commerce	Print Express	The Upperton Company	733801	1,425
Vacant					**111,025**
850	Commerce	Vacant	Metropolitan Consolidated	Vacant	4,500
855	Commerce	Vacant	Federated Dept Stores	Vacant	80,000
860	Commerce	Vacant	860 Commerce Associates	Vacant	5,500
888	Commerce	Vacant	Revland Realty	Vacant	6,680
960	Commerce	Vacant	The Upperton Company	Vacant	8,660
970	Commerce	Vacant	The Upperton Company	Vacant	1,615
998	Commerce	Vacant	The Upperton Company	Vacant	1,120
1001	Commerce	Vacant	The Upperton Company	Vacant	2,950
	42.8% Percent Vacant			Total S.F.	**259,625**
				Percent Retail	48%

Table 4.1

Phone or Direct Phone produce CD-ROM databases from which a downtown organization can generate listings of firms in its district. These listings will usually have one or more SIC numbers for each firm. Although these databases are usually at least six months out-of-date, they are very useful for constructing a database of downtown commercial space because they provide a computerized listing in which most items will be correct and the erroneous ones can be easily corrected in the field. Using pre-existing databases such as these is usually significantly cheaper and easier than starting to build a downtown commercial space database completely from scratch.

Review Previous Market Research Studies. These may have used survey data, census demographic data or business data. Studies done more than five years ago should be treated with caution, but still may provide interesting clues about niches.

Conduct a Shopper Intercept Survey. If done properly, this can be a useful tool for identifying trade area boundaries and existing niches. But, all too often, intercept surveys are amateurishly done, with bad sampling techniques, poor questionnaires, untrained field staffs (who are often teenagers) and low proportions of completed questionnaires/interviews among the shoppers who are asked to participate. Problems can be generated by such issues as: where the shoppers are to be intercepted; whether the field staff is biased (even if unintentionally) in whom they select to intercept; the time it takes to complete the questionnaire; and the intrusiveness of the individual questions asked. Also, a shopper intercept survey will tell you nothing about people in the trade area who are not shopping downtown. Field experience in a number of downtowns suggests that intercept surveys yield the best results when they are well-focused on obtaining a limited amount of information, perhaps asking no more than about 10 questions. However, when intercept surveys are properly performed, they can be very useful and can be accomplished for a reasonable price.

Conduct a Trade Area Survey. A survey of trade area residents is one of the best ways to identify a downtown's existing niches. Such a survey should investigate the types of goods and services trade area consumers actually come downtown to obtain. Surveys are a much maligned research tool because too many are improperly done. Questionnaires cannot be "ripped off on the back of an envelope." Samples must be scientifically selected and be of a size to assure the desired level of accuracy at the desired level of confidence. The interviews must be conducted professionally. The cost of a reliable telephone survey of trade area residents will depend on the number of completed interviews desired, and the number of questions that will be asked. A survey with more than 360 completed interviews is recommended. A useful, if minimalist questionnaire can translate into interviews that take at least five minutes to complete; an ambitious questionnaire can easily result in interviews lasting between 10 to 15 minutes. Still, for between

$8,000 and $15,000, a downtown can expect to get a very useful and reliable survey of its trade area's residents conducted by an experienced, reputable survey research firm.

No matter what kind of data you have, in analyzing how to find existing niches, the primary objective is to identify significant economic strengths that might exist in your downtown. These might be evidenced by such indicators as:

- the number of shops in a particular economic area of activity such as food for the home

- the total amount of commercial space occupied by that economic activity

- the economic activity that draws the most people downtown

- the amount of annual sales in a particular economic activity

- a combination of all of the above

One of the most important things to remember is that *the purpose of finding existing niches is to facilitate your downtown organization's promotional, marketing and business recruitment campaigns. These niches already exist, you do not have to create them — your challenge is to get the existing niches organized and active.* Consequently, do not feel constrained by such things as SIC categories, although they can be an admittedly useful and vital tool. For example, one downtown's home furnishings/home center niche contains firms outside of the two-digit SIC 57 furniture and home furnishings category, with some falling into the SIC 52 building materials category and others being in the SIC 59 miscellaneous retail group. Shoppers wanting to improve their home might be interested in going to an art gallery, frame shop, and brick and tile store even though the government doesn't classify these economic activities in the same category.

Likewise, downtown Rutland, VT's wedding niche brings together travel agents, florists, printers, men's and women's clothing stores, jewelers, restaurants, caterers, etc. This niche not only crosses retail SIC categories, it also includes those in the service industries. The advantage of this niche to the Rutland Partnership is precisely its ability to bring together many diverse downtown business operations so they can benefit from a joint promotional and marketing campaign.

Downtown Rutland's attempt to develop a Soho niche[99] will in similar fashion bring together another group of diverse business operators: restaurants, brew pubs, coffee houses, craftsmen, artists, cinemas and a legitimate theater. They will all be bound together by an ambiance that projects a special atmosphere comparable to the Soho area in lower Manhattan, which is home to many artists and galleries.

While there is certainly nothing wrong with finding out that your downtown has a restaurant niche, a women's specialty clothing niche or a "big box" discounter niche, at times these niches may be modest in size and leave many other downtown businesses "niche-less." Frequently in such situations, by using a little imagination, an existing downtown niche can be conceptually enlarged to include other business operations that otherwise would be niche-less. Since the strength of a downtown organization usually increases with its ability to include more and more businesses in effective promotional and marketing campaigns, it is usually in its best interest to enlarge existing niches so they can cover downtown businesses that otherwise might be loners.

Naturally, this can be taken too far and result in large niches which are so abstractly defined that they are hard to "operationalize" by building and running effective promotional and recruitment programs for them. For example, a downtown organization trying to work with a niche based on "comparison shopping" in a promotional and advertising campaign would find that it would have as little impact as using a niche defined as "downtown retailing." It would be analogous to Madison Square Garden advertising itself to sports fans as a sports arena instead of advertising the basketball or hockey games that are played there.

2. *Identifying Potential Niches.* In a sense, a downtown's potential niches are not real or tangible because there are few, if any, firms in them. A potential niche, at its core, is nothing more than a feasible market opportunity for attracting the firms that would create an "existing" niche. Creating a niche can be even more challenging than trying to organize an existing niche. A lot is likely to be at stake, including your downtown organization's reputation and the success of very large investments made by the public and/or private sectors. While the benefits of creating a new niche can be very substantial — for example, new niches can definitely turn a downtown around — it is critical to reduce risks by correctly identifying market potential for and feasibility of the new niche.

Spin-Offs of Existing Niches. Often, having one niche provides the foundation for developing another one, since one niche provides potential customers for the other. For example, if a downtown has a significant amount of office space, then it might be reasonably expected to also develop a business services niche to supply the firms in these offices with restaurants and delis to provide meals for their employees, especially at lunch time.

A lot of children's clothing stores can indicate an opportunity to attract toy stores and children's educational operations; they also can indicate an opportunity to develop a stronger women's clothing niche (since women are very likely to be the ones making purchases for children) that both targets their mothers and has shops featuring styles and sizes for their grandmothers.

Westfield, NJ has a very attractive and walkable downtown. The downtown is unusual for a town of its size, since it is not a linear strip, but a number of streets comprising a compact core area. The downtown already has a significant restaurant niche, but downtown leaders are considering the development of a performing arts center and the recruitment of "performing" craftsmen to establish a broader niche based on entertainment. Such a niche would encourage more evening strolling and window shopping, making good use of this downtown's walkable layout.

Look at Your Downtown's Characteristics. As Figure 4.1 demonstrates, a downtown's existing characteristics can indicate possible new niches (in this instance, for office space). Notice that the term being used here is "characteristics" and not "assets." This is because characteristics is a broader term, encompassing

---

Look Again At Your Downtown's Characteristics And Their Market Implications

- Courts and government offices: lawyers, public management consultants and software writers, architects, nonprofits
- Hospitals: doctors, dentists, medical labs, biomedical sales offices, biomedical start-up firms
- Universities: business incubators, conferencing
- Nearby airport: freight forwarders
- Very good interstate highway access: regional sales offices
- Attractive old bulding stock: professionals, start-up firms
- Many unemployed, highly skilled managers and engineers: start-up business

Figure 4.1

---

things that from one perspective may appear to be a liability, but that from another perspective may be an asset. An illustration: Many communities have suffered from high unemployment rates, especially among highly skilled managers and engineers, but these are precisely the people who are starting new companies in droves and who are very likely to appreciate downtown business locations. Think of how Eureka, CA took problematic second-story spaces to provide residential workplaces for a new artists' colony or of how Peekskill, NY used empty factory buildings to develop the same type of niche. Notice, also, how the artists then became the basis for developing or growing restaurant niches in both communities. Many downtowns have run-down waterfronts or abandoned railroad stations — liabilities that can be turned into very strong assets.

Look at Niches in Comparable Downtowns. Once again looking at successful niches in other downtowns can be a good indication of what might succeed in yours. Generally, it is a very good idea for a downtown organization to identify three of four comparable downtowns in its region and for the staff and board members to make periodic field visits to them. Much can be learned from such visits — about niches as well as other issues of interest to the downtown organization.

Discovering Untapped Niches Through Market Research. Just as with discovering existing niches, market research can be very useful when trying to identify untapped niches. Trade area surveys can regularly identify the goods and services for which residents feel under-served. Surveys can also be used to provide similar information for other key consumer groups such as downtown workers and tourists.

A type of market research that compares estimates of how much local consumers spend on various types of goods and services (demand) with estimates of the dollar value of the downtown sales of these goods and services (supply) can be another very good way to identify possible niches.

Focus groups are another useful tool for *identifying* the potential niches a downtown might develop. This research tool is best for getting *qualitative* types of results, such as ideas about possible niches. It has little real quantitative value: For example, you cannot assess the size or strength of a potential niche market through focus groups. The use of focus groups is most frequently abused when attempts are made to extract quantitative conclusions from them. On the other hand, focus groups are extremely useful in the construction of survey questionnaires, or to structure other research which is suitable to use for estimating the size and strength of a potential niche market.

A Word About Trade Areas

One of the most important concepts and tools that is used in identifying potential niches and assessing their viability is the trade area. A trade area is the geographic area from which specific kinds of customers come. There can be trade areas for residential shoppers, downtown workers or downtown overnight visitors. A primary residential trade area for comparison shoppers goods might represent the areas from which a downtown retail center gets 60 to 75 percent of its residential shoppers. A downtown office worker trade area can be defined as the geographic area from which a shop might be expected to attract 80 percent of the people who work in local office buildings. Unfortunately, in a large number of downtown market analyses, the trade area's boundaries are wrong! *And because the boundaries are off, the analysis of the trade area is also usually wrong!*

1. *A Downtown Usually Has a Number of Trade Areas, Not Just One.* Many analyses of downtown retail markets discuss only one trade area — which then may be broken down into primary and secondary sectors. In fact, a downtown may have many different trade areas, such as:

- a primary trade area for convenience goods, such as those sold in groceries, drugstores, card shops, etc. (usually areas that are within a seven- to 10-minute travel time of the downtown)

- a primary trade area for comparison shoppers goods (places which are 20 minutes by car from the downtown)

- a primary trade area for a factory outlet center (places that are 40 minutes or more by car from the downtown)

- a primary trade area for a retail niche (places that are as far as 20 to 40 minutes by car from the downtown)

2. *The Adoration of the Radii.* If you contact a firm selling demographic or business data, they will often ask whether you want the information for a one-mile, three-mile or five-mile radius. You might even request data for a 10-, 20- or 40-mile radius. Because of the ease of obtaining data in this way, many analysts use a radius to define a downtown trade area. The problem is that *trade areas are very rarely — if ever — circular in shape!* This is demonstrated by Figure 4.2, which shows the primary "upscale" trade area of downtown Englewood, NJ, for its home center and specialty women's clothing niches. Notice the irregular shape of this trade area and the fact that downtown Englewood is not even at the center of it. Observe also that, had a radius been used, the trade area might have included communities on the other side of a very wide river, although the river in fact serves as

Englewood, NJ — Home Furnishings Trade Area

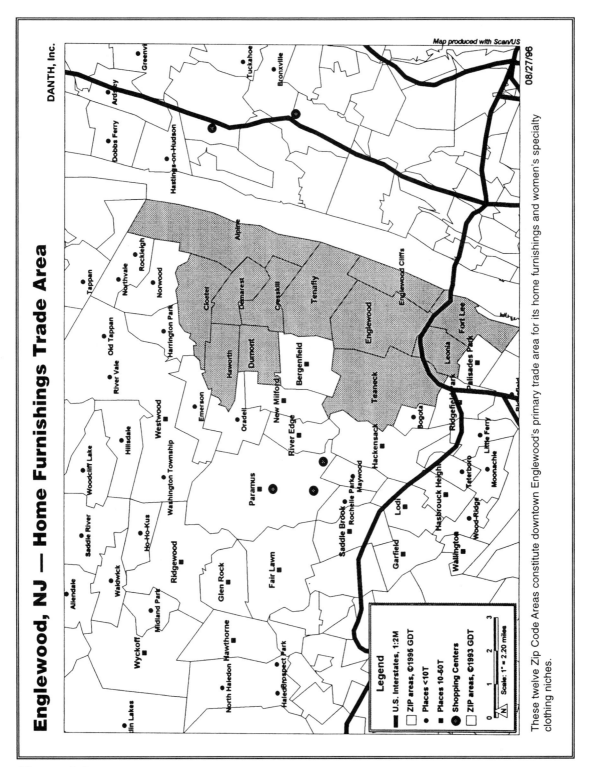

These twelve Zip Code Areas constitute downtown Englewood's primary trade area for its home furnishings and women's specialty clothing niches.

Figure 4.2

Englewood, NJ — Convenience Trade Area

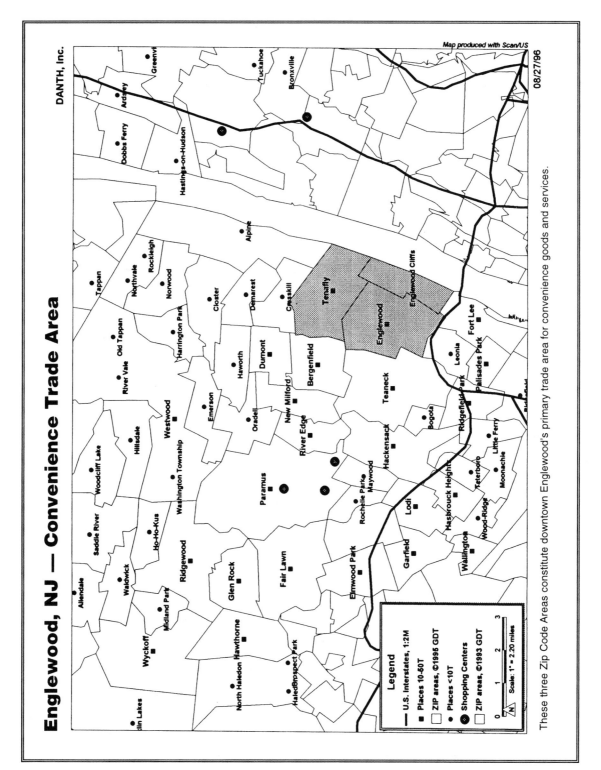

These three Zip Code Areas constitute downtown Englewood's primary trade area for convenience goods and services.

Figure 4.3

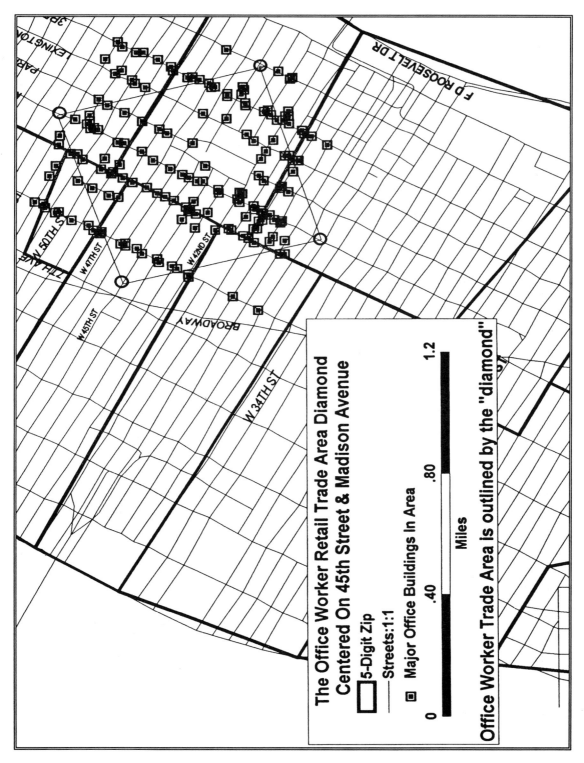

The Office Worker Retail Trade Area Diamond
Centered On 45th Street & Madison Avenue

5-Digit Zip
Streets:1:1
Major Office Buildings In Area

Miles

0   .40   .80   1.2

Office Worker Trade Area is outlined by the "diamond"

Figure 4.4

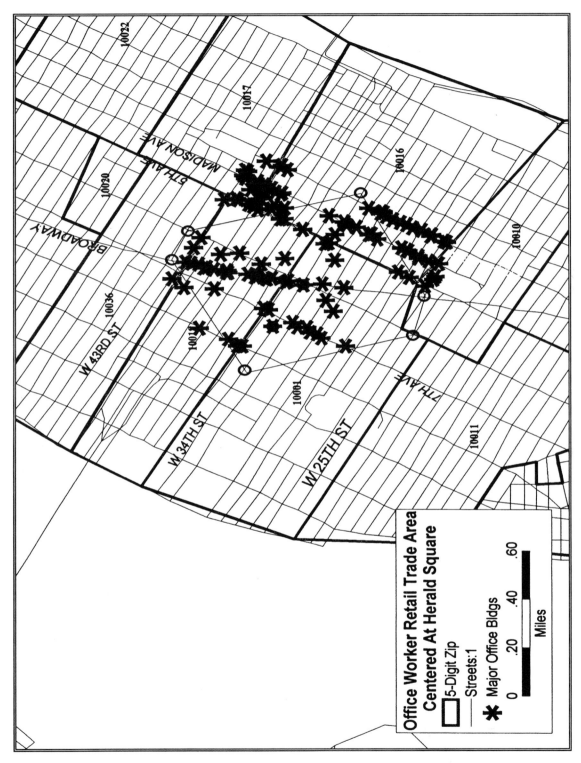

Office Worker Retail Trade Area
Centered At Herald Square

☐ 5-Digit Zip
— Streets:1
✳ Major Office Bldgs

0 .20 .40 .60
Miles

Figure 4.5

an effective moat deterring shoppers on the other side from coming to downtown Englewood. Figure 4.3 shows downtown Englewood's primary trade area for groceries and convenience goods and its size is considerably smaller than Englewood's trade area for its home center and specialty women's clothing niches.

A downtown's residential retail trade areas are usually very closely related to some portion of its transportation shed. They are also frequently influenced by socio-economic factors such as income, race, religion, age, etc., as well as lifestyle patterns. Incomes and lifestyles, for example, explain a lot about the shape of the Englewood trade area.

Downtown office worker trade areas also are often inaccurately described by a circle. Figure 4.4 shows the office worker trade area for shops located at the intersection of 45th Street and Madison Avenue in Manhattan. Notice that it has a diamond shape, which is a result of the area's rectangular street grid. Figure 4.5 shows the office worker trade area for shops located on Herald Square. Here, because of the impact of Broadway, which cuts diagonally through the area, the "tips" of the diamond are snipped off.

Many tenant prospects, especially retail chains, use and may ask downtown organizations to provide demographic or business data for an area encompassed by some radius. Experience suggests that downtown organizations which provide their own definitions of their trade areas as well as the relevant demographics for them, will have a more favorable impact than those who comply with radius-based data. The area circumscribed by a radius around a downtown frequently will include communities or neighborhoods that generate few if any downtown visitors, but they have attributes that can detract from the downtown's image if they are associated with it.

3. *How To Define Your Residential Trade Areas.* Two good methods for defining your downtown's current trade areas for residential shoppers are:

- *Intercept Surveys.* These were discussed above. It is a good idea to try to get 1,000 or so completed interviews that include the Zip Codes within which the respondents reside. A number of GIS (geographic information systems) such as Scan/US have the ability to geo-code data by Zip Code. This can be a quick and easy way to graphically identify and represent your trade areas.

- *Mailing Lists and Charge Lists.* These can be very useful because they can show where shoppers are coming from by type of store (for example, housewares, food, women's apparel). Many shops — even small independents — keep such data in a computerized format. Also, some credit card companies, such as American Express, will generate reports for shopkeepers listing Zip Codes for their customers using the card. A problem with these types of data is that there is often no way to distinguish between customers who work downtown and those who are residential shoppers from the trade area. Because many downtown employees can live beyond a downtown's residential trade area, this can lead to an exaggerated definition of its boundaries. Again, the use of a GIS such as Scan/US, MapInfo Desktop or Maptitude can be a big help in mapping and analyzing these kinds of data.

An analysis of potential niches might also want to look at "potential trade areas" — towns or neighborhoods from which the downtown might be expected to attract shoppers but, in fact, does not. Such an analysis can show how a downtown's sales can be increased by expanding the geographic area from which it draws most of its residential shoppers.

Perhaps the most basic tool for identifying a potential residential trade area is an analysis of the downtown's travel shed. People reasonably might be expected to travel seven to 10 minutes by car for convenience goods and 20 minutes for comparison shopping goods. The contours of a trade area defined by travel times are never circular because of the distances between main roads, differing actual road speeds on them, the time drivers need to get to them, and the impacts of such things as bridges, hills and congestion.

A comparison of the existing trade area and the potential trade area can be very revealing as shown in Table 4.2. This table shows that there is a substantial amount of incongruity between the current primary residential trade area for comparison shoppers goods of downtown Upperton, NY[100] and its 20-minute-by-auto travel shed. The current travel shed was defined using information provided by downtown Upperton's three main anchors, which are all nationally known department stores.

The Zips which are within a 20-minute drive of the downtown, but not in its current trade area — e.g., xxx03,xxx04, etc. — should be analyzed further to determine why retailers are not capturing shoppers from these Zip Codes.

The Zip Codes that are within the trade area even though they are more than a 20-minute drive from the downtown also are of interest, since an

	The Impact Of Auto Travel Time On The Extent Of Downtown Upperton's Primary Residential Trade Area		
Zip	**Part of Zip Within 20-Minute Travel Time**	**Trade Area**
xxx01	100%	in
xxx02	100%	in
xxx03	100%	out
xxx04	100%	out
xxx05	100%	in
xxx06	50%	in
xxx07	0%	in
xxx08	0%	in
xxx09	0%	in
xxx10	10%	in
xxx11	100%	in
xxx12	100%	out
xxx13	0%	in
xxx14	100%	out
xxx15	100%	in
xxx16	100%	in
xxx17	35%	in
xxx18	100%	in
xxx19	20%	in
xxx20	100%	in
xxx21	0%	in
xxx22	0%	in
xxx23	100%	out
xxx24	100%	in
xxx25	100%	in
xxx26	100%	in
xxx27	100%	in
xxx28	0%	in
xxx29	20%	out
xxx30	100%	in
xxx31	65%	in
xxx32	90%	in
xxx33	55%	in
xxx34	0%	in
xxx35	100%	in
xxx36	70%	out
xxx37	100%	out
xxx38	100%	out
xxx39	70%	in
xxx40	0%	in
xxx41	100%	in
xxx42	100%	in
xxx43	0%	in
xxx44	35%	in
xxx45	100%	in
xxx46	65%	in
xxx47	15%	out
xxx48	25%	out
xxx49	60%	out

Source: PEC Associates; DANTH, Inc.

Table 4.2

analysis of them may indicate downtown strengths that have gone unrecognized.

A telephone survey of residents in these crucial Zip Code areas can be an invaluable analytical tool.

Assessing Niche Viability

Having identified an existing niche or a potential new niche still leaves a lot to be done before an effective niche strategy can be completed: The niche's viability[101] must be assessed. Much has to be learned about each niche, since each can be impacted by many factors that will determine whether or not it can be successfully expanded or newly developed in a specific downtown. Moreover, some of these factors may be unique to that particular niche. The discussion below is not intended to be exhaustive, but will focus on some of the most important factors.

1. *Assessing the Market Strength of a Niche.* This is a very important step and preferably should involve an analysis of both supply and demand. Table 4.3 shows an example of such an analysis that was performed to assess the possible expansion of a restaurant niche in the Cedar Lane Special Improvement District in Teaneck, NJ.

The household expenditure data are based on information gathered by the Bureau of Labor Statistics of the U.S. Department of Labor. Sales figures are from the Census of the Retail Trades, which is conducted every seven years by the Bureau of the Census. The unmet demand may be treated as an indicator of an untapped local niche — in this instance, for merchants on Cedar Lane.

1993 Food Away From Home New York MSA ZIP 07666- Teaneck			Prepared for the Cedar Lane SID 11/17/95	
1993 Households (Estimated): 13,210				
		Expenditure Per Household		Total Expenditures
food away from home	$	2,217.40	$	29,291,857
beer/ale away from home	$	57.93	$	765,255
wine away from home	$	40.49	$	534,873
other alcoholic beverages away from home	$	89.65	$	1,184,277
Totals	**$**	**2,405.47**	**$**	**31,776,262**
Sales of eating and drinking establishments in 1992			$	18,568,000
Unmet demand			$	13,208,262

Source: BLS, Scan/US, DANTH, Inc.

Table 4.3

While it may be preferable to look at both the supply and demand sides of a niche, the instances when this will be possible unfortunately are not that frequent. Opportunities to include both demand and supply factors will exist when a niche's definition is consistent with the way the Census Bureau codes its business data and the categories the Bureau of Labor Statistics uses in its household expenditure studies. Secondary manipulations of Census or BLS data to make them fit niche definitions are very likely to have very significant error factors — and these are likely to be compounded when the results of one data manipulation are added to another.

Sometimes, information about supply is not necessary. For example, Table 2.3 on page 24 shows an analysis of under-served demand for specialty foods which uses survey data combined with data on expenditure potentials. This type of analysis reveals the level of consumer dissatisfaction with existing retailers and indicates how much market share is "up for grabs" — that is, new and more competent competitors can potentially win this market share away from current retailers.

Table 2.5 on page 28 is based purely on the results of a trade area survey and it provides information about the size of the demand for various entertainment activities in the trade area of downtown White Plains. Note that here the unit of quantification is not expenditure dollars, but the frequency of engaging in the relevant activities. Also note that a key finding is in terms of how many people want to do more of each specific activity in the downtown. Even though dollar amounts are not involved, such analyses of "traffic" or activity levels can frequently be very informative when the goal of the analysis is to assess the size and strength of a potential downtown niche.

2. *The Need for Appropriate Commercial Space.* Another critical factor in determining a niche's viability is the availability of suitable space. What is a suitable space for one niche, may be entirely unsuitable for another. As we have seen above, artists require spaces that are relatively large and inexpensive for them to both work and reside in. But these artist's spaces are quite different from the 50,000 SF to 70,000 SF that a modern competitive supermarket might require. And the artists and supermarkets will require quite different kinds of space than "lone eagles" who are looking for a telework facility.

In addition, the space should have the appropriate amount of parking for that niche. Some retail and office functions might require as much as five parking spaces per 1,000 SF, while others may have far lower parking needs.

Similarly, some niches will have a strong need to be very close to mass transit or major interstate highways, while, for other niches, the need for these location features will not be as strong.

The important thing is to find out what kind of space is desired by firms active in the niche(s) you are interested in nurturing in your downtown. If your downtown has such spaces, then it has important existing assets for developing these niches. The viability of a niche increases with the number of appropriate potential downtown locations for its businesses. If your downtown does not have such locations, you must determine whether or not they can be developed. The development of this space then becomes a key element in your downtown's niche strategy.

For illustrative purposes, Figure 4.6 shows the results of a research project formulated to learn about the types of locations biomedical and health care firms prefer for new office or research facilities. Obtaining information about the space requirements of firms in most niches typically will not need a research effort of this magnitude and usually can be achieved by talking to a limited number of knowledgeable real estate brokers, developers and executives from firms in the targeted niche.

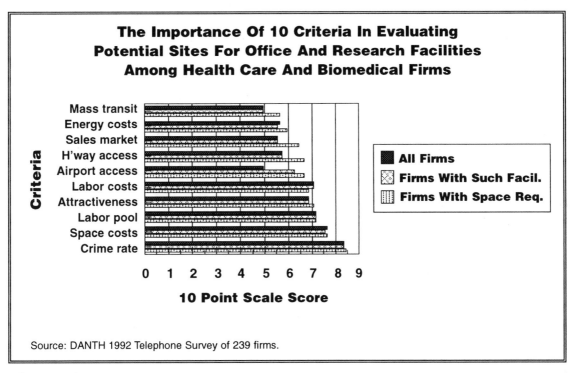

The Importance Of 10 Criteria In Evaluating Potential Sites For Office And Research Facilities Among Health Care And Biomedical Firms

Criteria (top to bottom): Mass transit, Energy costs, Sales market, H'way access, Airport access, Labor costs, Attractiveness, Labor pool, Space costs, Crime rate

Legend: All Firms; Firms With Such Facil.; Firms With Space Req.

X-axis: 10 Point Scale Score (0 1 2 3 4 5 6 7 8 9)

Source: DANTH 1992 Telephone Survey of 239 firms.

Figure 4.6

3. *The Importance of Who Lives Downtown and in Nearby Neighborhoods.* One of the factors that will have the greatest impact on the viability of developing a new niche or expanding an existing one, is the people who live in and around a downtown (in its core trade area). These trade area residents, because they are so close, will not only come downtown frequently to shop for comparison shoppers goods, but also to:

- shop for convenience merchandise

- visit professional services such as doctors, lawyers, accountants

- use personal services such as dry cleaning, beauty parlors, shoe repair shops, day care

- visit business services such as banks, loan companies, copy shops, stationery stores

Consequently their visitation rates to the downtown will be significantly higher than people living in other parts of the primary trade area. And because they visit so often, core area residents are very likely to account for an extremely high percentage of downtown pedestrians. Consequently, their consumer tastes and social behaviors on downtown streets and in public spaces will have a powerful impact on the area's image.

This point is demonstrated in Figure 4.7 which shows how many times a month residents in the primary trade area of Bergenline Avenue in West New York, NJ visited various shopping centers. While non-Hispanics visited Bergenline Avenue more often than any other shopping area, their visitation rate paled in comparison to the Hispanic trade area residents, who averaged over 10 visits a month. One reason for this is that 110,478 (or 86 percent) of the primary trade area's 116,722 Hispanics live nearby in the core area. This situation helps explain why Bergenline Avenue has developed its reputation as a major Hispanic shopping area.

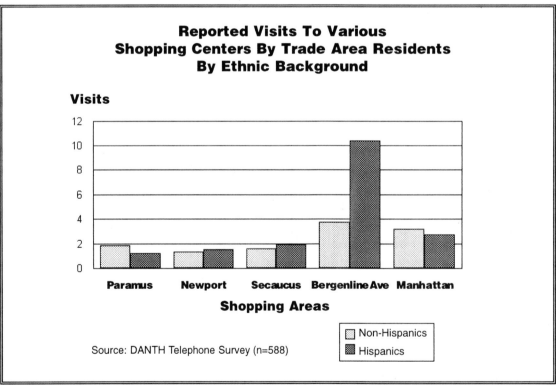

Figure 4.7

It also helps to explain why area merchants have been unable to build a retail center that attracts the comparison shopping dollars of the area's high-income households (which average more than $60,000 per year) located about one mile away.

4. *Local Political Support*. If local merchants or residents vehemently oppose a particular downtown niche, then it is very likely that plans for its development or expansion will fail. A successful niche strategy will be crafted to carefully consider potential opponents and tailored to either assuage or combat them.

Current Firms in a Niche. Frequently, opposition to the expansion of a niche comes from the downtown businesses that are already operating in it. The usual basis for their opposition is the fear that attracting additional firms to the niche will mean a cannibalization of the market and reduced sales for their stores. Usually, these business operators do not understand the strengths of agglomeration and specialization, and consequently cannot appreciate the benefits of having a robust niche.

There is no guaranteed way of dealing with this type of situation, but a downtown organization will be more likely to be persuasive if:

- it has a history of good communications with these business operators

- it has run a good educational program to indoctrinate downtown business people about niche strategies and why they are critical to the downtown's growth and survival

- the opponents can be shown examples of large, robust and successful downtown niches

- there is a detailed, credible market analysis showing that an expanded niche will mean increased sales for both the niche as a whole and the individual firms within it

General Opposition from Downtown Business Operators. In recent years, such opposition has tended to occur when there are proposals to develop a value retailing niche based on power centers, "big box" retailers (Wal-Mart) and/or "category killers" (Home Depot). But savvy downtown organizations can make a very credible case for welcoming these "900-lb. retail gorillas." Admittedly, it may take a lot of time, money and effort to carry the day, as well as a history of good communications between the downtown organization and the merchants. Some key arguments for welcoming the 900-lb. gorillas to downtown might be:

- The adverse competitive effects of these 900-lb. retail gorillas usually are not avoided by preventing them from coming downtown. They simply will locate elsewhere in the trade area and thus adversely impact downtown merchants.

- While there is little doubt that some shops will be put out of business by these retail giants, their precise number will depend on how many downtown merchants respond appropriately to the new competitive pressures and find their own niches — that is, the parts of the market that the 900-lb. gorillas are not serving. It will also depend on their ability to band together as a unit to conduct joint advertising, promotions and business recruitment campaigns. *But, once the 900-lb. retail gorillas appear on the scene, downtown retailers must face these pressures to change and adapt whether or not the gorillas locate in the downtown.*

- On the other hand, large retailers are precisely what most downtowns need because they can substantially increase customer traffic. As Dick Courcelle, the executive director of the Rutland Partnership, argues, the new Wal-Mart in his downtown will expand the size of downtown's trade area and lengthen its business hours to seven days a week, 9 a.m. to 9 p.m. But downtown retailers must know how to take advantage of that increased traffic.[102]

Research performed for downtown White Plains, NY supports Courcelle's contention. There, the very successful 870,000-SF Galleria Mall has sales per square foot that place it among the top one percent of super-regional malls in the nation. Yet there has been a general perception among downtown White Plains' merchants, property owners, realtors and shoppers that on-street retailing was struggling with reduced customer traffic, a weak store mix, low-quality merchandise and significant vacancies. Many on-street merchants blamed the mall for their predicament.

A comprehensive telephone survey of trade area residents, which paid particular attention to residents in the core trade area, found that 63 percent of the Galleria's shoppers also shopped in the on-street stores (see Table 4.4). The survey also found that 67 percent of the respondents from the core area rated the on-street shops as poor or fair while only 32 percent rated them as excellent or good. Residents in the core area, who visit the downtown more often and know it better, tended to have a harsher view of the on-street stores than trade area residents who live further away (see Table 4.5).[103]

Where Trade Area Residents Shop In Downtown White Plains			
	Core	**Outer**	**All**
Only the Galleria Mall	20.7%	18.8%	19.8%
Only street-level shops	20.9%	15.8%	18.7%
Both	34.5%	15.5%	26.2%
Neither	23.9%	50.0%	35.2%
Percent of Galleria Shoppers Using street-level shops	62.3%	45.2%	57.0%

Table 4.4

How Trade Area Residents Rate Street-Level Shops In Downtown White Plains			
	All	**Core**	**Outer**
Excellent	2%	3%	2%
Good	31%	29%	36%
Fair	43%	43%	44%
Poor	19%	24%	12%
Don't know	4%	2%	7%
Total	99%	101%	101%

Table 4.5

A detailed analysis showed that core area residents may have one or two on-street shops that they frequent, despite their negative perceptions of most on-street shops. One has to wonder how much more often the core area residents who shop in the Galleria would shop in the on-street stores and how much more money they would spend in these shops if the on-street merchants would provide higher quality goods, better service and a more attractive shopping environment.

Traditionally, small merchants have not been known for their willingness to accept change. The threats posed by the 900-lb. retail gorillas to their livelihoods and ways of doing business in effect create a crisis situation for them. A downtown organization can help small merchants adapt to this need to change by providing them with an appropriate niche strategy and technical assistance on the merchandise and services they should offer and ways to improve their own marketing.

Opposition from Local Residents. Disappointed expectations can be a major cause of opposition by local residents to the development of a particular niche. Local residents, to cite just one instance, may have a very proud and positive image of their community and believe that they deserve shops of commensurate quality, but the realities of the market may conflict with these expectations. The residents may object to a niche which does have market viability, but does not match their image of their community. For that reason, the proposed niche's viability may well depend on the downtown organization's ability to educate the residents and make their expectations more realistic.

For example, in Upperton, NY,[104] an opinion survey as well as views voiced at several public meetings all indicated that residents wanted high-end retailers such as Nordstrom's, Tiffany's and very fashionable boutiques to be recruited to their downtown. While the community had an estimated median household income in 1995 in excess of $80,000, in the surrounding communities the median household incomes were $20,000 to $40,000 lower. Unfortunately, Upperton's population is not big enough to support the kinds of retailers local residents want, and its downtown must compete with almost 3.8 million SF of competitive retail space located along the town's borders.

Residential opposition can also be aroused by the specific development projects that implement a niche strategy. For instance, supermarkets are often a major anchor for a food-for-the-home niche, but in many communities nearby residents have objected on the basis of too much increased traffic, sanitation problems with refuse and the visual appearance of the market being in conflict with surrounding residential and commercial buildings. In fact, a properly planned supermarket can deal with each of these problems and can, for example, be so attractive and conform so well with downtown storefront design that it looks nothing like a traditional strip mall supermarket.

A downtown organization considering new commercial projects to implement its niche strategy would do well to anticipate possible residential opposition and to make plans for dealing appropriately with it. Photographs of similar projects in other downtowns and computer-generated graphics showing how the proposed project would actually look and interact with its surroundings — combined with appropriate consultations with community groups — can be powerful tools for mobilizing residential support.

It is also a very good idea to have alternative sites identified for such projects. However, it should be kept in mind that alternative sites are seldom equally suited for a particular project.

5. *Niche-Specific Factors.* Almost every niche has one or more factors that uniquely affect its viability. To construct a viable niche strategy, it is essential to learn about these factors and to properly take them into consideration. These factors demonstrate the need for researching a niche beyond the point of gaining a grasp of local levels of supply and demand and getting an understanding, in effect, of how it operates. The discussion below will focus on a few dissimilar niches and is meant to be illustrative, rather than exhaustive.

The Office Worker Niche. Many assessments of the downtown office worker market commit a gross error in research design by simply identifying the number of people who work in a downtown's office buildings and then trying to estimate their demand for various goods and services. Such assessments ignore at least three pivotal factors:

- how far office workers will travel on their lunch hour

- the amount of time office workers have for lunch

- how many cafeterias/lunch rooms downtown firms provide for their employees — often with food that is significantly subsidized

Based on survey research conducted for the International Council of Shopping Centers in 1988 and downtown consultant Larry Houstoun's very insightful analysis of its findings, we know that office workers in most downtowns do not walk farther than 1,000 feet on their noon-time trips. In the ICSC survey, 80 percent of the downtown office workers reported their usual travel time to a lunch-time destination as nine minutes, and 70 percent walk only one to three blocks. The 1,000-ft. figure is derived from these findings through the use of average walking speeds and the typical amount of time people need to leave and enter office buildings.[105]

In effect, this means that downtown retail locations will have office worker trade areas that are defined by a 1,000-ft. walking distance from their doors. Because of the size of many downtowns, this means that downtown will have many office worker trade areas, not just one.

It also can mean that retail locations just one block apart will be able to access office worker trade areas of very different sizes and sales potentials. This is demonstrated in Table 4.6, which shows how much occupied office space is located within a 1,000-ft. walking distance of two intersections in downtown White Plains, NY, which are located one block away from each other. As clearly shown, one trade area has more than double the amount of occupied office space than the other.

Downtown White Plains:
Major Office Space Within Two Office Worker
Trade Areas That Are One Block Apart

Intersection	Total Building Size (SF)	Total Occupied Space (SF)	Available Space (SF)
Mamaroneck Ave. and Main St.	3,007,892	2,328,276	679,616
Mamaroneck Ave. and Martine Ave.	1,243,594	1,020,910	222,684

Table 4.6

How much time office workers are given for lunch will impact significantly on how much time they have to walk to lunch-time destinations and how many tasks or errands they can complete besides obtaining their food. A half-hour lunch pattern obviously will provide a far less promising office worker retail market than a downtown in which the average office worker has one hour for lunch.

Similarly, when companies provide in-house dining facilities for lunch (and sometimes even for breakfast), this will keep office workers from going outside of the building and greatly diminishes their likelihood of shopping in downtown stores.

Tourism. Having a large stream of out-of-town visitors is no guarantee that downtown retailers will benefit from this potentially lucrative market. For example, a study done for Downtown Ithaca, Inc. found that the downtown's "...shopping opportunities need to be improved from the viewpoint of tourism."[106] Ithaca, NY (population 26,000) has many assets that generate a lot of tourist traffic: It is the home of Cornell University and Ithaca College; sits on the southern end of Lake Cayuga, the largest of the Finger Lakes; and has many beautiful state parks nearby. An important conclusion of the report was that:

"There is no point in attracting tourists if you do not have the goods and services to market to them."[107]

Among the report's recommendations is the suggestion that downtown Ithaca should try to provide a unique shopping experience that will stand out in the tourist's mind. Downtown Ithaca might achieve this with:

- more boutiques and upscale shops

- a stronger sense of a district, with a shopping opportunity built around a single theme rather than an *ad hoc* collection of independent shops

- a more "fun" shopping experience

For a variety of reasons, many other downtowns have found it very difficult to tap into the tourist market. For example:

- Skiers are often difficult to attract downtown because at the end of the day they are too tired to come down off of the mountain, or, the hotels they are staying at provide an array of dining and entertainment activities.

- The tourists might be heterogeneous in incomes and lifestyles, presenting a splintered market, the various parts of which by themselves cannot support local retailers.

- The tourist market, as a whole, is not large enough by itself to support local retailers and differs in lifestyle and income from the local residential market.

While the solution in Ithaca may be to provide more upscale retailing in a "fun" downtown environment, other downtowns may succeed in tapping the tourist retail market with other tactics. A good example is Lenox, MA (population 5,149). Lenox is the home of a major Shakespearean company at The Mount (the Edith Wharton estate), will soon be home to a new major national music center, and is the summer home of the Boston Symphony Orchestra at Tanglewood. The arts attract a huge number of tourists to Lenox, as evidenced by the strength of the local hospitality niche. Although Historic Lenox Village has attracted a Talbot's and a few other apparel shops, most of the retailing, exclusive of restaurants, in one way or another continues the "arts" theme. For example, there are gold- and silversmiths, furniture makers, a weaver, a shop featuring hand-crafted leather goods, art galleries and antique shops.

In contrast, about 70 miles north of Lenox on U.S. Route 7, is Manchester, VT (year-round population 3,622). The countryside around Manchester is an extremely popular four-season resort area that attracts many visitors and second home owners. The response of the business community in downtown Manchester to this fertile retail market has been the development of one of the most successful factory outlet centers in the northeastern United States: There are over 50 shops, including Burberry, Ralph Lauren, Baccarat, Jones New York, Brooks Brothers, Coach, Anne Klein, Timberland, Tse, Joan and David, Dansk and Orvis.

Ethnic Niches. Two very important, but often overlooked factors in the development of ethnic niches are the regional and crossover markets. Many ethnic niches are very strong because they have a very large nearby customer base — often within easy walking distance — which has stimulated the emergence of a large number of establishments catering to the tastes of the particular ethnic group. These ethnic niches are large and unique shopping centers. But, because they are either doing so well with just their local customers or they are unorganized, local ethnic merchants often fail to market and promote themselves to other members of their ethnic group who live in other parts of their region — say, within a 40- to 60-minute drive. These untapped regional markets can represent significant growth opportunities.

A good example of how a regional ethnic market can be tapped is the Yaohan supermarket chain. This Japanese chain has about nine stores across the nation, with a very popular one in Edgewater, NJ. The market benefits from Bergen County's significant Japanese population, but on the weekends its parking lot is filled with buses and automobiles carrying Japanese shoppers from all over the region.

Similarly, the new supermarket opening in Teaneck, NJ will use the significant number of Orthodox Jewish households in Teaneck and adjoining communities to provide the basic market support for a retail establishment that will be able to draw Orthodox customers from 14 counties in northern New Jersey.

The crossover market is composed of members of other ethnic groups. For a Latino niche, for example, the crossover shoppers are all non-Latinos. The successes of Chinatowns and Little Italy's across the country demonstrate the potential of this type of market.

Recent cultural trends suggest a growing crossover potential for other ethnic niches. For example, Americans are eating less meat and fat and consequently "America's health concerns are stoking the assimilation of ethnic flavors today."[108] And, according to a vice-president of the Campbell Soup Company, "consumers are turning away from processed-type products and the ethnic product embodies that fresher, unadulterated image they want."[109] Additional evidence is provided by the fact that since 1991, salsa has been outselling ketchup in the United States.

Non-food products also offer crossover opportunities. The resurgence of interest in cigars has led to a demand to visit high-quality cigar makers and to see cigars being hand-rolled. Such "cigar performance" shops are springing up in downtowns with large Cuban-American populations (for example, Coconut Grove, FL and Union City, NJ).

CHAPTER 5
NICHE ORGANIZATION, MARKETING AND PROMOTIONS

Firms in existing niches have an inherent tendency toward organization because of their deep-seated commonality of interest — that is, the kinds of goods and services they vend and the market segments they are trying to reach. This commonality of interest makes it easier to envision and agree upon marketing and promotional themes, advertising campaigns, special events and business recruitment programs. However, despite this proclivity, all too often firms in a niche do not become organized. Since being organized is essential to the creation and success of niche marketing, promotional and business recruitment programs, the discussion below first will review some of the factors that determine whether or not the firms in an existing niche can get their act together and become organized. Then, the discussion will focus on the wide array of niche advertising and promotional activities that downtown organizations are now using.[110]

Convincing Niche Firms to Organize

The Waynesville Antique and Merchant Advertising Association is a very good example of how the forces surrounding a niche push its firms towards organized forms of behavior. Waynesville, OH is just a small community of 1,950 people, but more than 30 shops in its antique niche have joined together in the Waynesville Antique and Merchants Advertising Association, which has been in existence since 1972. With no paid staff, it still manages to spend $18,000 to $20,000 a year on advertising. According to Linda Hoppe, its secretary-treasurer, the association uses a variety of advertising and promotional tools:[111]

- a billboard on I-71, the major highway linking Cincinnati, Columbus and Cleveland

- display ads in antique periodicals

- display ads in the major newspapers within its "90-minute market," i.e., those in Cincinnati, Columbus, Dayton and Indianapolis

- an Antiques Directory

- an Annual Antiques Show

The funding comes from voluntary contributions, which for many business operators constitute their entire annual advertising budget.

Downtown advertising and promotional programs based on voluntary contributions — usually a very unreliable revenue source — are notoriously insecure, often are short-lived, and struggle to be effective. So why is the Waynesville association successful? Why is it able to mount a program, using one of the most unreliable funding techniques, that many larger downtowns might envy?

The reasons appear to be that Waynesville antique dealers realize that:

- The local population is rather small and its expenditures alone cannot support them.

- To succeed they must tap a much larger market.

- The best way of tapping this larger market is by creating a real "destination" capable of attracting shoppers from considerable distances; and their niche constitutes this destination, offering customers a wide selection of merchandise within a very walkable environment — just like a specialized shopping center.

- For the niche to be marketed properly as a destination, they must band together in a common effort; no single shop could afford the program, and their very agglomeration demonstrates that they are a destination.

Clusters of antique shops or shops featuring other very highly specialized merchandise will have a very strong propensity to engage in organized behaviors because their primary trade areas are likely to be geographically very large. Consequently, there is a high probability that establishing the niche as a destination and using cooperative marketing and promotional efforts to successfully penetrate this market area will be seen by niche business operators to be natural, sensible and logical steps to take.

The awareness of the need to penetrate a new or larger market is generally one of the keys to successfully organizing firms in a niche. Conversely, organized behavior becomes problematic when the firms in a niche believe they are located in a "zero-sum" market situation, that is, one in which there is no growth and an increase in one firm's market share means a decrease in another's. Perceptions of a zero-sum market are the primary reason niche business recruitment programs are not more prevalent.

For example, Dick Courcelle, executive director of the Rutland [VT] Partnership, organized firms in downtown's wedding niche, but found organizing the restaurant niche a much more challenging task. Some restaurant operators were unwilling to participate in cooperative advertising and promotional campaigns aimed at diners living in downtown Rutland's primary trade area. The "hold-outs" believed that they had a pretty good grasp of the primary market area and felt it was rather mature. They consequently saw themselves as competing for the same static amount of dining-out dollars. Accordingly, they feared that "some other downtown restaurant might benefit from the money they contributed to a proposed cooperative niche advertising campaign focused on primary trade area residents, while they would not."[112] On the other hand, the restaurant owners were willing to participate in cooperative niche advertising programs aimed at attracting skiers from major nearby resorts, a large and potentially very lucrative market that downtown retailers have only recently begun to penetrate.

One of the reasons the Rutland Partnership had an easier time organizing the wedding niche was that those firms conducted such disparate activities that they did not perceive themselves as competing directly with each other.

Another very important factor was the realization among the firms in the wedding niche that by banding together they were creating a true downtown destination which would enable them to capture a much higher share of the wedding market. The Partnership also plans to market the restaurant niche heavily as a downtown destination to skiers. Courcelle wants skiers to feel that:

> "They don't need to have any particular restaurant in mind before they come downtown, because we have so many fine restaurants that they are bound to find one that they will truly enjoy."[113]

Niche organizations can take many forms, such as a merchants association, a local development corporation or a downtown district. Waynesville exemplifies the merchant association model. In Midtown Manhattan, the garment industry has formed the Fashion Center Business Improvement District and the jewelers along 47th Street have formed their own BID; both clusters had local development corporations prior to the creation of BIDs. Sometimes a BID that has a number of existing niches will create merchants associations and make them extensions of the district's organizational structure. For instance, downtown Red Bank, NJ has antique, restaurant, art gallery and florist niches. Tracy Challenger, executive director of RiverCenter, the downtown district, plans to create a merchants association for each niche to facilitate the participation of niche business operators and make it easier to manage niche programs.[114] And in Decatur, GA, the Downtown Development Authority helped to create the Decatur Restaurant Association because restaurant owners needed "to unite to create a cohesive effort and image."[115]

The fact that Rutland's Courcelle manages a downtown district and has managed to successfully organize two niches is indicative of the advantages such districts have in implementing niche strategies. Most importantly, downtown districts can provide the staff to work on organizing a niche — many niches go unorganized because no one is working to bring the firms together. They also can have a relatively assured budget that will allow them to offer financial incentives to firms participating in a niche advertising campaign or special event. Although, as demonstrated in Waynesville, a "niche organizer" can emerge without a district, as can an effective advertising program, such requisites for an active niche are more possible when a downtown district exists.

The fashion and jewelry clusters in Midtown Manhattan exhibit another strong stimulus for firms in an existing niche to coalesce and work together on a wide range of issues, projects and programs: the emergence of very serious challenges to their positions by outside competitors. The jewelry cluster along 47th Street is the largest in the world: At least 75 percent of the diamonds that entered the United States in 1995 — about $4 billion worth — went through the 2,600 diamond-related firms in this cluster. The dominance of this cluster now is being challenged by established centers in Antwerp and Tel Aviv as well as new ones that are emerging in India, Thailand and China.[116] Similarly, the Fashion Center BID was formed to help maintain midtown Manhattan's position as a major player in the world's garment industry.

Courcelle argues that having a niche development strategy based on solid market research is an invaluable asset in organizing niche firms. Besides helping to legitimate the niche approach, it can demonstrate:

- the new markets and growth opportunities available to firms in the niche

- the strength of the firms already in the niche and their ability to compete within this larger market

- how a niche can be used to create a powerful downtown destination

- how other niches have succeeded

As a result, it can be a downtown organization's most powerful tool for altering perceptions among niche business operators that they are in a zero-sum market situation.

Opposition to organizing a downtown niche is likely to come from three types of business operators:

- those who perceive themselves to be in a "zero-sum" market situation

- others who are very "insular" — they do not work with other downtown businesses, tend to feel that they can handle all of their problems by themselves, and want other downtowners to just leave them alone

- those who are content, feeling that they already have robust sales revenues and plenty of opportunities for growth

The difficulty of organizing a niche obviously will correlate strongly with the prevalence of such attitudes. If these types of business operators are very prevalent in a niche, they make a "bottom-up" organizational strategy almost impossible. A bottom-up strategy is one in which the organizing agent, in the form of a niche business operator, emerges from within the niche itself and convinces other business operators to act together in a concerted fashion. However, if there is a strong downtown organization (especially a special assessment district), it may still be possible for an effective "top-down" strategy to work in such a situation, although the going still can be expected to be tough. An effective top-down niche organizing strategy might involve:

- Assigning a staff person to meet with niche business operators and get them organized (the need for this is obvious).

- The creation of a niche development strategy based on good market research[117] (such a strategy can help change the minds of those with zero-sum market perceptions).

- A lot of public discussion and media coverage on the strategy (this demonstrates that the strategy is serious and worthy of attention).

- The endorsement of the strategy by the Board of Directors of the downtown organization (this legitimates the strategy and may stimulate some overly content business operators to "go along," especially if the costs are not too high).

- Forming a leadership group of pro-niche business operators and having them communicate with the hold-outs (peer pressure is an important means of influencing business operators; and hold-outs often can turn out to be niche leaders).

- If possible, organizing one or more field trips to downtowns where the niche strategy has worked.

- Including in the advertising or promotional campaign some small-scale elements that will not demand too much time or money (this will make it easier for the hold-outs either to "go along, in order to get along," or to "test the waters," at relatively little cost).

- Offering significant financial incentives by having the downtown organization assume a larger than normal share of the costs for the cooperative program.

- If possible, using a core group to run the campaign even if a substantial number of niche firms do not initially participate (such a campaign could demonstrate its effectiveness and show how it impacts favorably on all niche member firms).

Niche Marketing and Promotional Programs

Niches can and have engaged in a wide range of marketing and promotional programs. Such programs are critical to maintaining the existing customer base, attracting new shoppers and making the downtown more attractive to new niche businesses. Many are quite simple and relatively inexpensive; others are more complicated and have commensurately higher costs. But, as the examples of Waynesville and Rutland demonstrate, effective niche programs can be carried out by small- and medium-sized downtowns, as well as central business districts in big cities.

There is no hard and fast rule about the amount of money a merchant should devote to advertising. Two percent of a shop's annual gross sales is a common figure given; but for new businesses or businesses with much competition, the figure might be higher. So, a downtown niche might reasonably be asked to spend at least two percent of its annual gross sales under normal conditions, and perhaps even more for initial advertising efforts when the niche's image has to be established. Of course, in practice there is usually a difference between what merchants should spend on advertising and what they actually do spend; so it is best to treat the two-percent rule as the upper parameter of what might be expected from them.[118]

In general, special events should be expected to be self-sufficient through the use of sponsors, vendor fees, group advertising, admissions and other fees to participants. The only cost to the downtown organization should be that of paying for the staff to work on the events during work time. The municipality usually provides the police, public works and fire staff as part of the in-kind costs it absorbs to support downtown revitalization efforts. Up-front costs such as portable bathrooms, tents, traffic cones, security, and rented tables and chairs are built into the costs of the event and divided among the sponsors and participants. Event advertising should be cooperatively planned and implemented through the committee organizing the event.[119] Again, differences can be expected between how a special event actually operates and how it should be run, especially when the people in charge of the event are relatively inexperienced. But as a rule, it is reasonable to expect niche special events to be largely self-supporting.

A cautionary note: Many downtowns commit a grievous mistake when they start to advertise and promote to bring new shoppers downtown before they are really attractive and marketable. For example, some years ago one large Midwestern downtown held barbecues and other special events aimed at bringing people back downtown from the surrounding suburbs. However, because of conditions downtown, the suburbanites who were attracted usually went away convinced that the downtown was dirty, ugly and dangerous and that people should only go there when there were special events and, consequently, a lot of security forces on the streets. Like downtowns themselves, downtown niches should not be marketed and promoted until they are attractive and strong enough to be really competitive.

1. *Example Program: Rutland, VT.* The Rutland Partnership has developed one of the most sophisticated and robust niche marketing and promotional programs. After a consultant presented a retail revitalization strategy at a public meeting of the Partnership, it was discussed at later meetings and eventually endorsed by its board. Firms in the wedding niche were then invited to a meeting to discuss what they thought could be done to promote the development of a wedding center. They came up with the concepts for a wedding brochure and a bridal show. The Partnership's staff then developed the ideas for a niche logo and decal, as well as a customer database. The idea of using a tab insert in the *Rutland Herald* was a logical outgrowth of the need to advertise the bridal show.

Tab newspaper inserts are widely used in downtowns across the continent. Rutland's Bridal Show tab is unusual because of its niche orientation (see also the discussion of RiverCenter's program in Red Bank, NJ, page 99).

The Wedding Center Brochure. This 33-page color publication not only contains ads about the shops in the niche and a map showing where they are located, but also provides very useful information about:

- a wedding checklist

- a realistic schedule for the checklist

- the items in a realistic budget

- who pays for what

- Vermont laws about getting married (where to get a marriage license, who may perform a ceremony, etc.)

- using a bridal registry

In addition to being genuinely useful, this information demonstrates the need for shopping at all the diverse firms in the wedding center. While some

Figure 5.1

other downtown niches have printed materials that might be considered as a brochure, few, if any, are as comprehensive, useful and attractive as Rutland's.

The brochure has been distributed by shops in the niche as well as at the bridal show. The distribution in niche stores of information about the other shops in their niche is a very important behavior for niche business operators to develop. It indicates that the operators understand how a niche as a downtown destination is useful to them: That shoppers are more likely to return downtown when desired merchandise can be found in some downtown store, and that if the shoppers do not make a purchase in a particular shop on one shopping trip, they may on the next.

The $7,500 cost of the 5,000 wedding center brochures were co-oped, with the shops paying for their ads and the Partnership contributing some funds.

The Bridal Show. The success of the first show,

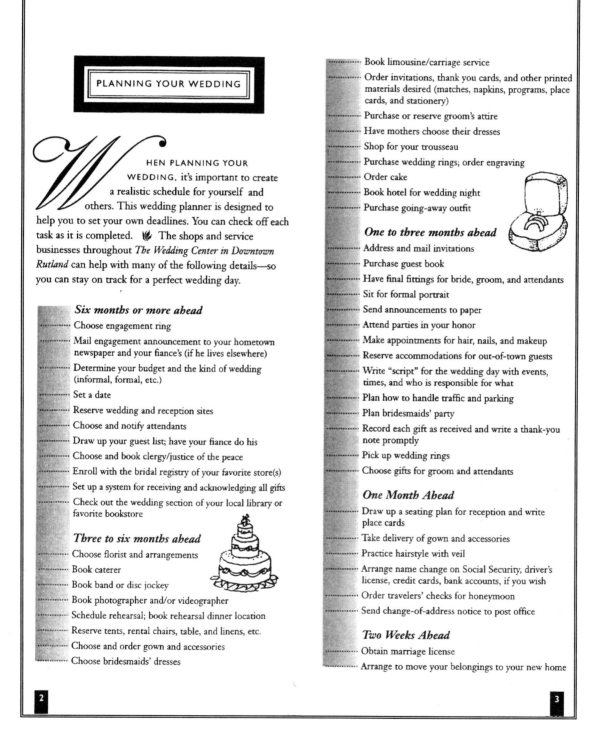

PLANNING YOUR WEDDING

*W*HEN PLANNING YOUR WEDDING, it's important to create a realistic schedule for yourself and others. This wedding planner is designed to help you to set your own deadlines. You can check off each task as it is completed. ❧ The shops and service businesses throughout *The Wedding Center in Downtown Rutland* can help with many of the following details—so you can stay on track for a perfect wedding day.

Six months or more ahead

- Choose engagement ring
- Mail engagement announcement to your hometown newspaper and your fiancé's (if he lives elsewhere)
- Determine your budget and the kind of wedding (informal, formal, etc.)
- Set a date
- Reserve wedding and reception sites
- Choose and notify attendants
- Draw up your guest list; have your fiance do his
- Choose and book clergy/justice of the peace
- Enroll with the bridal registry of your favorite store(s)
- Set up a system for receiving and acknowledging all gifts
- Check out the wedding section of your local library or favorite bookstore

Three to six months ahead

- Choose florist and arrangements
- Book caterer
- Book band or disc jockey
- Book photographer and/or videographer
- Schedule rehearsal; book rehearsal dinner location
- Reserve tents, rental chairs, table, and linens, etc.
- Choose and order gown and accessories
- Choose bridesmaids' dresses

- Book limousine/carriage service
- Order invitations, thank you cards, and other printed materials desired (matches, napkins, programs, place cards, and stationery)
- Purchase or reserve groom's attire
- Have mothers choose their dresses
- Shop for your trousseau
- Purchase wedding rings; order engraving
- Order cake
- Book hotel for wedding night
- Purchase going-away outfit

One to three months ahead

- Address and mail invitations
- Purchase guest book
- Have final fittings for bride, groom, and attendants
- Sit for formal portrait
- Send announcements to paper
- Attend parties in your honor
- Make appointments for hair, nails, and makeup
- Reserve accommodations for out-of-town guests
- Write "script" for the wedding day with events, times, and who is responsible for what
- Plan how to handle traffic and parking
- Plan bridesmaids' party
- Record each gift as received and write a thank-you note promptly
- Pick up wedding rings
- Choose gifts for groom and attendants

One Month Ahead

- Draw up a seating plan for reception and write place cards
- Take delivery of gown and accessories
- Practice hairstyle with veil
- Arrange name change on Social Security, driver's license, credit cards, bank accounts, if you wish
- Order travelers' checks for honeymoon
- Send change-of-address notice to post office

Two Weeks Ahead

- Obtain marriage license
- Arrange to move your belongings to your new home

2   3

Figure 5.2

held in 1995 (more than 230 people attended, with over 35 exhibitors), led to another show in 1996. The Partnership's staff was responsible for putting the show together. Costs were covered by the exhibitors and by sponsorships. Niche firms reported a very significant increase in wedding-related sales and many, as a result, increased the lines of wedding-related merchandise they carried.

Downtown Rutland's bridal show is fairly unique because, being based on a synthetic niche, it brings together many downtown businesses that otherwise would not have any organizational umbrella under which they could promote and advertise themselves.

The Bridal Show Rutland Herald Tab. Because of the ads being placed by bridal show participants, the *Rutland Herald* donated editorial space so that one of its tab inserts focused entirely on the bridal show and bridal center. (See more about tabs in the discussion on page 99 on Red Bank's niche advertising.) The tab was distributed to the *Herald's* entire readership.

Figure 5.3

The Bridal Center Logo and Decal. Because most downtown niches are not physical clusters, it is important for them to find a way to indicate to downtown shoppers that the niche exists. In addition, Rutland's wedding center had the problem of not being intuitively apparent because of the diverse activities it brought together. This could also make it difficult at times to perceive the niche in print advertising. The Rutland Partnership's solution to these problems was to design a logo for the wedding center to be used on a decal in shop windows to denote niche membership. The Partnership also distributed logo slick sheets and offered partial reimbursement to niche members when they included the wedding center logo in their independent print advertisements. Although the reimbursement offer has not proven to be as successful as hoped, the Partnership's staff believes that the concept is valid and plans to review ways of increasing its use.

The Customer Database. The list of names, addresses and telephone numbers of the people attending the bridal show constituted a list of "qualified" customer prospects: Their attendance provided strong evidence that they were in the market for wedding-related goods and services. The list also contained information about wedding dates and the future spouses' names and addresses — which increases the reach of this list. Such lists are of great value to retailers. The Rutland Partnership took the information from the bridal show and, at relatively little expense, made it available to the firms in the wedding center in PC-readable format. The firms in the niche could thus easily contact these customer prospects by direct mail.

Nationally, downtown retailers — large or small — are finding it very useful to generate similar lists from their sales and charge slips, as well as by providing a guest book where shoppers can place their names and addresses and ask to be placed on the shop's mailing list. The power of these lists could be increased significantly if firms in a niche would share them.

2. *Example Program: Waynesville, OH*. The main components of the Waynesville program were briefly described earlier in this chapter. The following discussion will highlight why the advertising and promotional activities of these antique dealers are relevant to other downtown niches across the country — besides the fact that so much is being done in such a relatively small community.

The Billboard. This form of advertising is often overlooked by downtown organizations, either because it has simply been forgotten or because of aesthetic reasons. However, billboards can be a very effective way to advertise, as indicated by the fact that in Waynesville a significant portion of the antique association's advertising budget is used to rent the billboard.

Ads in Antique Periodicals. Advertising in targeted publications increases the probability of reaching the consumers who are most likely to be interested in your niche. The Waynesville antique association uses antique periodicals and magazines; many niches in other downtowns also might benefit from advertising in specialty publications. Depending on the geographic areas they cover and whether their advertising can be targeted to particular geographic areas, special interest publications can be an effective way to reach potential tourists with interests that mesh with a particular downtown niche. Specialty publications that are fairly local or regional can provide excellent opportunities to reach a targeted audience at an affordable price. Many metropolitan areas across the country, for example, have magazines named after the core city (for example, *New York, Dallas, Los Angeles,* etc.). These publications often have a readership with vestigial Yuppie tendencies: They are affluent, comparatively young and interested in the latest trends in dining, entertainment and fashion and, consequently, are an audience that several obvious niches might want to reach.

Antiques Directory and Map. This is a very simple and handy publication, which is basically an 8-1/2" x 11" piece of paper which folds into three panels. It serves a very basic and important function that every downtown niche must have performed: Identifying the names of the shops in the niche and informing the shopper where they are located and how to get to them. It is distributed in all of Waynesville's shops.

The directory portion is clearly presented and easy to read. The map uses three different symbols to distinguish between antique shops, specialty shops and food and lodging. Additional information about downtown Waynesville is conveyed in a single page, but because this commercial area is relatively small, the reader is able to find out easily what shops are there and how to get to them.

Almost every downtown has a map and the vast majority of them are dismal failures because they try to convey so much information in a comparatively small space, making the map difficult to read. One explanation is the desire to show how much is located downtown. Whether this is the proper function for a map is debatable. What is certain is that maps that are confined to displaying the shops in a particular niche are generally the best for niche business operators, especially as the number of all downtown shops often ranges from about 100 to past 300. The map of the restaurants on Lincoln Road Mall in Miami Beach, FL shows how much clearer and more direct a niche map can be (see Figure 5.5).

Display Ads in Major Regional Newspapers. That the Waynesville association has a fairly sophisticated understanding of its market area is demonstrated by its use of these ads. The 90-minute market is probably its trade area and these newspapers may be the best means of reaching residents interested in antiques.

Full-page downtown niche ads in newspapers are rare finds, but many more downtown niches could be doing them. Full-page display ads by downtown organizations in major daily papers are not rare, but they usually are not niche-oriented and feature shops of all kinds. In downtowns with a number of niches, advertising campaigns that rotate full-page display ads highlighting different niches might prove to be very effective.

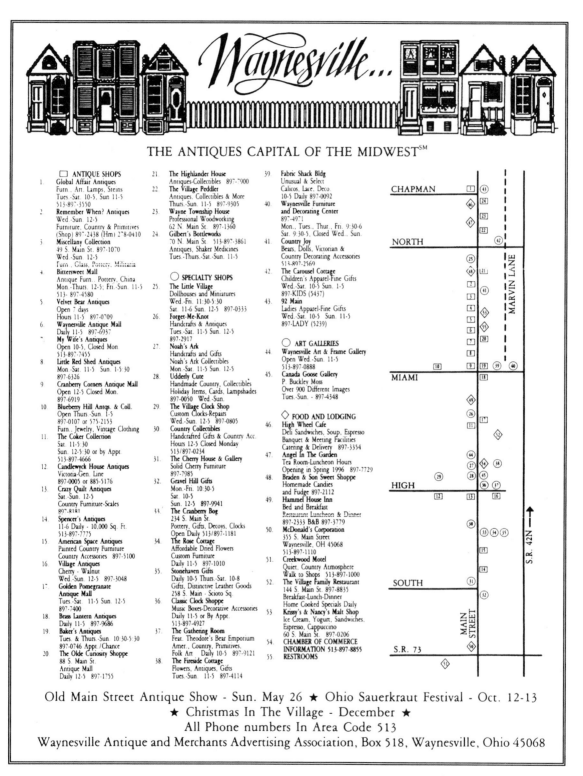

Figure 5.4

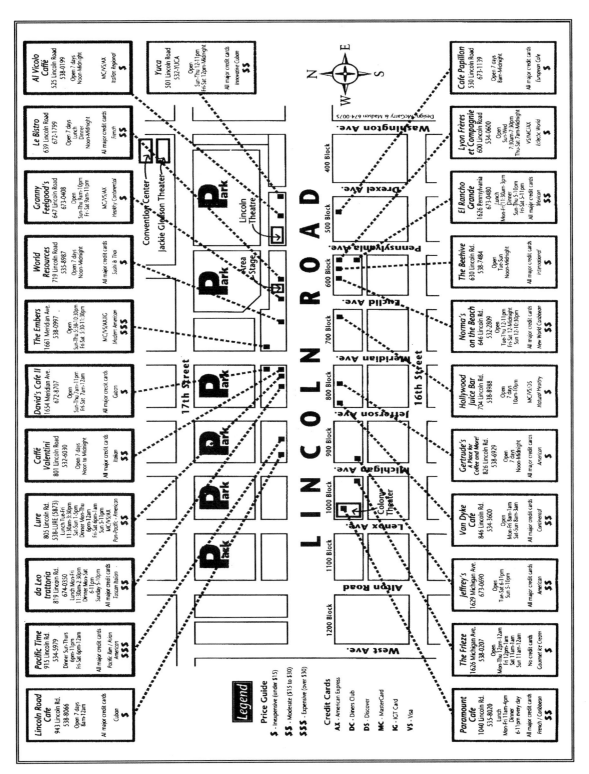

Figure 5.5

Cost is an obvious factor influencing the use of this type of advertising and it can vary considerably by publication. For example, on Long Island in New York State, the cost of a one-page ad in a strong local weekly paper with a circulation of about 10,000 would be $1,051. If, under a co-op program, a downtown BID paid half of the cost ($525), then 10 niche merchants could split the remainder at the cost of $52 each. A similar ad could be placed in an edition of *Newsday* targeted to a portion of Nassau County that probably has a population exceeding 250,000 for about $1,620. Under a BID co-op program, 10 niche retailers would pay $81 each to participate. If the ad was placed in the Long Island Section of the *Sunday New York Times*, which covers a three-county area having a population of several million people, the costs would be significantly higher. The cost of a full page is $6,000 and higher graphic design costs would be anticipated. If a downtown BID paid half of *The New York Times* cost ($3,000) and covered the graphics design cost, 10 niche merchants could split the remainder of the cost at $300 each.

Perhaps more important than cost is the fit between a niche's trade area and a publication's readership. As was mentioned earlier, downtown niches often have different trade areas and so some, such as food for the home, might find the weekly paper best, while others featuring comparison shopping goods would find the targeted *Newsday* ad the best for reaching their potential customers. Niches with very large trade areas, such as antiques and value retailers, might find a major regional paper like *The New York Times* best.

Annual Antique Show. This has been held for the past seven years on Memorial Day weekend. Outside dealers are invited to participate.

Events such as an antique show can bring in many new shoppers by increasing the penetration of the existing trade area as well as bringing in visitors from beyond its boundaries. If antique dealers can hold such shows, then perhaps firms in other niches that need a fair amount of space to display their merchandise, such as furniture and home furnishings, could do so as well.

3. *Example Program: Red Bank, NJ.* Downtown Red Bank, NJ has a number of strong and very sophisticated marketing and promotional efforts to support its jewelry, restaurant and antique niches, but perhaps of equal interest is the way that many other organizations have become deeply involved in these projects.

Riverfest. For the past 15 years, downtown Red Bank has held a food and music event in the spring which has grown into a major attraction drawing well over 100,000 visitors over three days. Attendees come from all over New Jersey and surrounding states. Organized by the Red Bank Chamber of Commerce (now known as the Eastern Monmouth Area Chamber of Commerce), in its first year it was called the Red Bank International Food Festival with only seven restaurants participating. Music that year was provided by a disc jockey and everything was held under one tent. In sharp contrast, the 15th Riverfest had 24 restaurants participating and non-stop jazz and blues music performed by 21 musical acts over the festival's three days. Each restaurant has its own tent. The music is coordinated by the Jersey Shore Jazz and Blues Foundation and has become a major attraction for jazz aficionados.

Admission is free, with visitors paying only for the food they eat and the activities they engage in. The event has attracted sponsorship from the Riverview Medical Center, Bell Atlantic NYNEX Mobile, Coca Cola, the New Jersey Lottery and NJ Transit.

The Downtowner. Many downtown organizations across the country have learned the value of using "tab" (for tabloid style) inserts in the local newspaper. These self-contained inserts combine articles about the downtown with advertisements for downtown shops and their suppliers. The tabs are not only distributed to the newspaper's readership within a targeted area, but they can also be distributed separately by direct mail to residents, and dropped off at local shops and office buildings. They also can make a great recruitment piece to send to office and retail tenant prospects. Generally, the only cost to a downtown organization for the tabs is some staff time and possibly a consultant to write the downtown news stories. The ads pay for the tab. However, if the tab is not going to attract more ads than usual from downtown businesses, then the newspaper will be reluctant to run it. In such instances, the downtown organization may consequently want to "guarantee" the tab, thus reducing the costs for each advertiser and making the whole venture more attractive to the newspaper.

The *Downtowner* is the tab for downtown Red Bank. It is printed seven times a year by the *Two River Times* in cooperation with RiverCenter, the organization managing the downtown special district. It now has a print run of 50,000 copies, more than double the original, and an estimated readership of 145,000. *The Downtowner* differs from many other downtown tabs in how it is distributed: In addition to the 34,950 newspaper inserts, 3,050 copies are delivered drop-point/bulk[120] and 12,000 copies are delivered by direct mail.

For many downtowns, especially those trying to reach affluent households, direct mail can be the best way to achieve their advertising objectives. In Summit, NJ, for example, the Promotions Committee of Summit Downtown, Inc. sends copies of their tab, *The Summit Collection*, to 60,000 homes.

The *Downtowner* is also notable for the amount of space it has devoted in ads and articles to niches. For example, one issue focused heavily on the jewelry niche, providing a map, an article on its history and development, ads by the jewelry shops and advertorials about them. In other issues, ads appear focusing on such subjects as "Where to Find Food in Red Bank" or "Red Bank: Antique Capital" that list the names and addresses of shops in each niche.

The *Two River Times* also produces niche guides, such as "A Guide to Red Bank Eateries" (see Figure 5.7), inserted in *The Downtowner*. These guides contain a directory of the shops in the niche, a map and advertisements for the niche shops in a handy, stand-alone format.

4. *Physical Signification of a Niche*. Business operators in a niche sometimes feel it is important for them to physically denote the niche's existence. As mentioned earlier, the wedding center in Rutland, VT is using a logo decal in shop windows to physically indicate its presence. Many other non-cluster niches may want to follow this precedent. Many clusters, however, also have some kind of physical indication of their existence. For example, Chinatowns in San Francisco, Philadelphia and Washington, DC all have some statue or gateway at their main portal. In Philadelphia, Jewelers' Row has hung street banners proclaiming its existence, and in Midtown Manhattan the new Diamond District BID plans to erect four 30-foot pylons topped by a Plexiglas model of a 57-facet diamond to denote the east and west entryways to the district. Since it is usually fairly easy to discern a cluster area, one may wonder why these clusters have this need to physically signify themselves. Some possible explanations:

• to "decorate" the area and improve its physical appearance

• to provide a sort of "caption" for the area

• to impart the feeling that the cluster is not an accident, but (at least in part) the result of organized human effort

• to identify boundaries and maintain property values

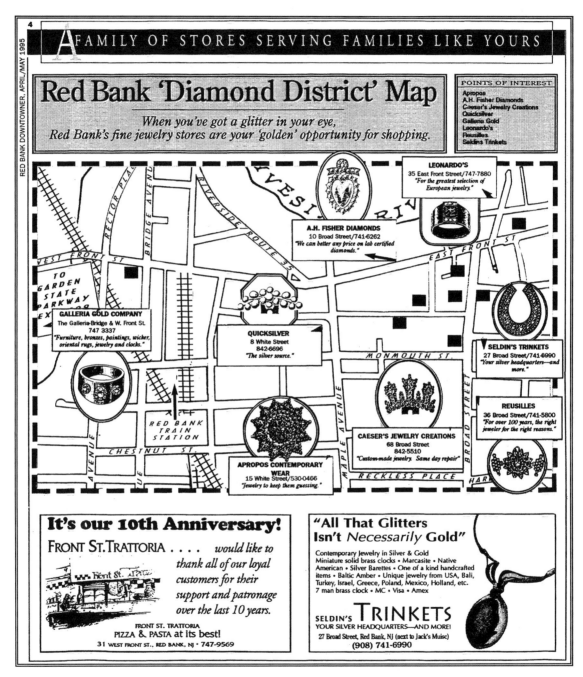

Figure 5.6

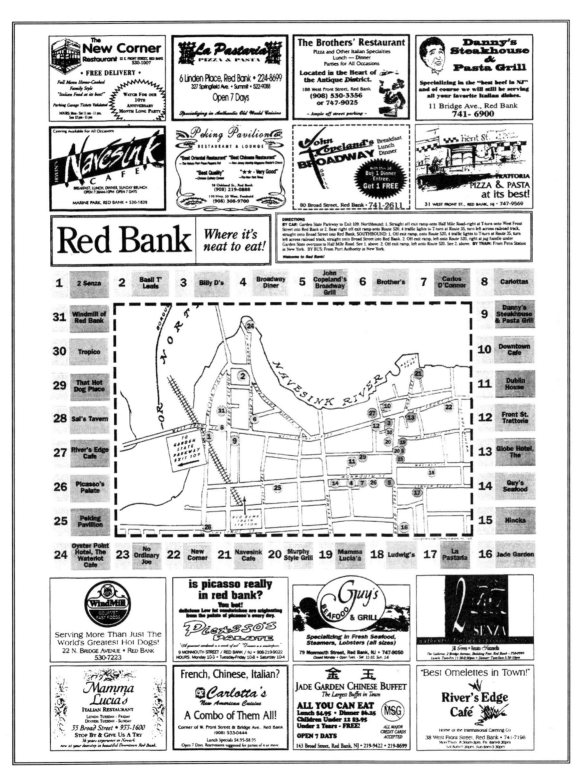

Figure 5.7

Whatever the reason, the results can be pleasing to the eye.

Downtowns having a number of niches may want to use the banner idea, rotating the niches on the banners over the year or alternating them along the street.

5. *Tourism: Cultural Institutions and Learning From Malls — The Cezanne Exhibit.* Perhaps the most important special downtown event in the past decade has been the Cezanne exhibit at the Philadelphia Museum of Art, which was held in summer 1996. While there has been a growing realization of the ability of cultural attractions to attract tourists, the manner in which the Cezanne exhibit was packaged, advertised and promoted promises to have a great impact on the way other cultural institutions, be they large or small, will do business. The museum spent $175,000 to advertise the exhibit in New York, Baltimore and Boston — cities located along the Northeast transportation corridor. For a nonprofit organization this is a very large advertising budget. There was also a 20-page special advertising section in *Business Week* magazine and a PBS program about the exhibit. The museum not only mounted an unusually large advertising and public relations campaign, but also worked with 15 major downtown hotels and many top-rated restaurants, such as Le Bec-Fin, to provide a very attractive package to tourists that included competitively priced rooms, free parking, discounted dinners and tickets to the exhibit that allowed entry at any time when the museum was open. The exhibit was a sell out, attended by more than 500,000 people. Many of them were from out-of-town. About 40 percent of the visitors who rented hotel rooms to see the exhibit came from New York City.[121]

As a result of the success of the Philadelphia Museum of Art's campaign, New York City's Metropolitan Museum, the Museum of Natural History and the Museum of Modern Art agreed to a joint advertising campaign that would also focus on major cities in the Northeast corridor.[122] None of them alone could afford such a campaign, but by pooling their resources they can.

Besides demonstrating how cultural events can have powerful economic impacts for arts and cultural niches, the other major lessons that may be drawn from the success of the Cezanne exhibit in Philadelphia are:

• You must put together a good product to sell to tourists.

• The product not only includes the cultural component, but hotels and restaurants as well.

- Offering a package deal makes it a lot easier for busy people to make all the arrangements to travel to your downtown; therefore, they are far more likely to come.

- Cultural institutions, hotels and restaurants have strong overlapping interests when it comes to tourism, so coordinating and partnering their efforts will usually result in higher revenues for all.

- A major product, properly packaged, can penetrate a large tourist market area, but properly advertising and promoting the product can be expensive; joint campaigns drawing resources from various sectors and lines of economic activity are probably required.

- Downtown organizations perhaps can stimulate tourism best by serving as a catalyst for these joint efforts helping to produce an attractive product and raising the funds needed to effectively market and promote them.

Malls and Tourism.[123] Shopping malls have learned that tourism can constitute a major portion of their customer base, accounting for between 25 to 44 percent of their revenues. As they became more aware of this market, shopping center managers and owners have developed marketing and promotional techniques that many "malls without walls" (that is, downtown retailers) might find instructive.

First, and perhaps foremost, the tourist-savvy malls know that their tenants have to be educated about this market. They do so through newsletters, meetings, workshops, etc. The Grand Central Partnership and the 34th Street Partnership in Midtown Manhattan are trying to follow this lead by undertaking serious campaigns to educate their retailers about the tourist market, especially through articles in their newsletters. Here again, market research can help convince downtown retailers about market opportunities.

One of the main themes behind the malls' techniques is the development of relationships and partnerships with other organizations. For example, shopping centers develop good relationships with motor coach operators, drivers and tour operators because motor coaches can bring in a lot of tourist traffic. Many shopping centers, such as South Coast Plaza in Orange County, CA, give free passes for mall restaurants and discounts for mall stores to motor coach drivers. The Chicago Place mall has managed to be the only designated motor coach stopping station in downtown Chicago, so all motor coaches going to downtown Chicago must stop there.

Another basic tactic is to build similar close relationships with hotel concierges and bellmen. This tactic is used by Horton Plaza in San Diego, as well as South Coast Plaza. Concierges and bell men can have a big influence on where tourists decide to go. These two malls also have developed co-marketing programs with many hotels' management. Horton Plaza has developed a shuttle service for hotel guests that brings about 2,400 tourists each month to its doors, with half of the cost of the shuttle being absorbed by the hotels and the other half by major mall department stores.

Partnerships with other organizations are also possible. South Coast Plaza has developed them with:

- car and bus rental companies

- other attractions such as Disneyland, Queen Mary and Spruce Goose

- meeting planners

- tour operators

- travel agents

Getting involved in travel industry associations and programs can lead to many important contacts and the opportunity for good public relations opportunities, as well as exposure to important market segments. One example: South Coast Plaza is now being packaged by Walt Disney Travel.

South Coast Plaza's success also makes the argument that a good media marketing plan — which is part of any overall marketing strategy — can result in great media exposure in such publications as *Vogue* and *Sunset* magazines, as well as being included in major tour guide books such as *Fodors*.

Savvy malls also know that penetrating the tourist market means that special customer services must be provided. For example, Chicago Place has:

- multilingual directories and interpreter services

- a full-time concierge to provide shopping, dining and cultural information and make reservations for dining and events

- free next-day delivery within five miles of the mall

At South Coast Plaza, the shops also have bilingual sales staffs, complimentary gift wrapping and free shipping.

6. *A Taste of (enter the name of your downtown here)*. This is a popular name for a special event that is held in many downtowns. It is one of the best ways to highlight a downtown's restaurants, food stores or caterers in downtown's food niche. Usually held in a large covered area with open walls or in booths placed along downtown streets, the event provides space to local restaurants that prepare and serve mini-portions of their best dishes.

Stowe, VT. A good illustration of this concept takes place in late July in downtown Stowe, VT. There, an ice skating rink is transformed into a large indoor area where the restaurants set up and serve. To make the event even more special, local artists set up an art show in the area as well. Attendees enter the art show for free but pay $.50 per ticket to buy samples of the food. One ticket will buy you a small dish; two or more tickets purchase a bit of something more special. The proceeds go to an agreed-upon charity which helps promote the event through its supporters and members.

Burlington, Ont.[124] This downtown has an annual walking tour of downtown restaurants. It is usually held on Saturday afternoons — restaurants tend to get busy Saturday evenings. Ten groups of 20 people are toured through 12 downtown restaurants. Volunteers from the downtown business improvement association serve as guides. Each restaurant prepares its specialty and many are linked with a nearby winery or brewery. The event is self-supporting, with the restaurants, wineries and breweries covering the cost of food and drink.

Cincinnati, OH. This is one of the oldest and largest "tasting" events in the nation, with the 16th being held on Memorial Day weekend in 1995. Over 52 restaurants in an eight-block area participated. Each has its own booth where it cooks and serves sample-size helpings of the house specialties. Each delicacy costs $2.50. Country, blues, rock, and jazz performances add a very popular musical element to the festivities. In 1995, over 500,000 people attended this event. It is organized by the Downtown Cincinnati Council and the Greater Cincinnati Restaurant Association.[125]

Dayton, OH. Downtown Dayton runs a Taste of the Miami Valley event which is similar to, but smaller than, Cincinnati's. About 30 restaurants are assembled in booths on Courthouse Square for one day.[126]

Springfield, MA. The Taste of Springfield has been a successful downtown promotion for 10 years. It is operated by the downtown's Bay State shopping center.

Murfreesboro, TN. The Taste of Murfreesboro is a sit-down dinner in downtown restaurants in which a tastings menu features the house specialties. Funds raised by this event go to Main Street Murfreesboro/Rutherford County to support downtown projects.

Milwaukee, WI. The Milwaukee promotion is also held in downtown restaurants. Tickets can be purchased individually or for a whole table. These "Gold Plate Club" tables also receive celebrity wait service by local sports, TV and radio personalities, plus special table settings and recognition in the program.[127]

7. *The Movies: Film Festivals and Late Shows.* These events and promotions can provide a big lift to downtown entertainment niches, not only benefiting the movie theaters involved, but also nearby restaurants, coffee houses, ice cream parlors, pubs, bars and nightclubs.

Festival content can have a big impact on the audience it attracts, often with unintentional consequences, so this is an important factor to consider. For example, a Midnight Madness festival of horror movies is likely to attract a teenage audience that will deter more mature movie fans from attending. Still, when programmed properly, film festivals can be important downtown events even in communities of relatively modest size. Many festivals try to focus on themes close to the cultures and histories of their cities and the major ethnic groups that live in them: The festivals thus become celebrations of the community.

Sarasota, FL. This downtown has three film festivals. The Project Black Film Festival centers on the theme of African-Americans and the African Diaspora. In 1996, it had its fourth annual run and now draws a loyal group of 5,000 film-goers. The festival attracts about an even number of white and African-American viewers and according to the festival's director, "It's an opportunity to promote cross-cultural understanding."

Decatur, GA. This four-day film festival runs adjacent to the annual Decatur Arts Festival. It is booked by a local filmmaker and focuses on films reflecting the experiences of the American South. Held in the public library, the festival is an entirely volunteer effort. The downtown organization believes that the film festival draws a "whole different group of people" to downtown film and cultural activities. The festival organizer convinced downtown businesses to designate a "post-screening hang-out," where film-makers could meet with film-goers over coffee after the screenings.

Many downtown organizations — such as the Bryant Park Restoration Project in Midtown Manhattan and the Halifax, Nova Scotia Downtown Business Commission — hold their film series and/or festivals in attractive outdoor parks. These events attract picnics, and are an excellent way to show off downtown parks and public spaces.

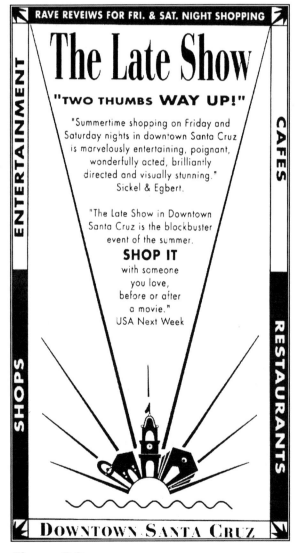

Figure 5.8

The Late Show In Santa Cruz, CA. After a new nine-screen cinemaplex opened, the Downtown Association of Santa Cruz began a promotional campaign aimed at convincing café and restaurant owners as well as other retailers that the movie theater would be bringing in a lot of potential customers on weekend nights and they should consequently stay open later on those evenings. The campaign also sought to convince the public that there would be more exciting things to do downtown on Friday and Saturday evenings. After a slow start, enough stores were convinced to participate to launch a major TV and print ad campaign. One shopkeeper reported over 150 customers in his store between his usual closing hour and 10:30 p.m. Other anecdotal reports suggested that many other restaurants and shops also saw a significant increase in their customer traffic during this promotion. The Late Show promotion is a good example of how one part of an entertainment niche can be used to build a promotion that will increase the customer traffic for other participants in that niche.[128]

8. *Office Workers.* Since office workers are a major niche in many downtowns, be they large or even fairly small, special events focusing on this key downtown consumer group have sprouted up across the country.

Figure 5.9

Louisville's Employee Appreciation Week. Every October, the Louisville Central Area, the downtown association and the downtown Louisville Galleria shopping mall organize a week-long event aimed at increasing purchases made by downtown workers, raising awareness of the variety of goods and services available downtown, and ensuring that employees enjoy working in and frequenting the central business district.[129] More than 80 downtown companies participate in the event. Employees are supplied with special coupon books containing over 70 offers and, in 1994, over 5,275 coupons were used. Employees are also invited to enjoy such attractions as:

- free-donut breakfasts

- a murder mystery dinner cruise

- a theatrical production

- musical events

- a wind-up party (in 1994, this attracted more than 400 people)

Joliet, IL. Under a variety of names, such as a "downtown office party" or "after hours," many downtowns have staged events for office workers that involve the following basic model: An after work activity in which a relatively modest sum — such as a $3.00 admission fee — is charged to get an office worker into the reception area (a parking deck, parking lot, mall lobby, office lobby, city green, restaurant or hall). Free food is available from downtown restaurants and food stores. Live music and recorded music encourages dancing and mingling. Beer, wine and soda are available for a cost. Joliet, IL[130] claims the world's largest office party with thousands of attendees each year. Dozens of downtown businesses offer coupons and promotions free of charge. The percentage of downtown sales to office workers has steadily increased since the first event.

Portland, OR. In 1993, the Association for Portland Progress, in conjunction with the Downtown Retail Council, started an annual Downtown Worker Appreciation Week that echoes the Louisville program. During an entire work week, workers are given a variety of services, admissions and merchandise at discounted costs. The workers identify themselves by their business cards or by an event lapel label they receive from their employers.[131]

9. Car Shows. America's love for the automobile is legendary. Many downtowns have found that car shows, whether they feature classic cars or new ones, can draw large crowds and be very successful. Many downtowns have clusters of auto dealerships and these events can be used to promote them. In October 1996, for example, downtown Englewood, NJ had a car show in which 15 dealers participated, displaying over 100 models. Other firms involved in the automobile business, such as suppliers and banks making consumer car loans, also joined in the event.

Most of the classic events are organized with the help of car clubs. Because they involve "old" cars, the shows can also be tied in with an antiques niche as in Carlisle, PA. Classic car shows can also be good for downtown entertainment niches. Enjoying the weekend events, participants in classic car shows also like to engage in a "Sock Hop" on Saturday night and listen to the "golden oldies." People who own classic cars tend to have expendable income and, contrary to what you might think, number men and women among their ranks. While downtown, both male and female car aficionados have plenty of time to shop and eat. They also rent hotel accommodations for the weekend.

A classic car show typically involves anywhere from 50 to 500 vintage cars parked along downtown streets or in downtown parking lots. It takes place over a weekend and usually involves:

- a twilight car cruise on Friday night

- the "show and shine" contest Saturday during the daytime

- awards followed by a "Sock Hop" Saturday night

- a pancake breakfast and play or travel time on Sunday[132]

Coeur d'Alene, ID, Traverse City, MI and Walla Walla, WA have all held very successful shows of this kind. The one in Traverse City reportedly led to a significant number of new downtown visitors who continued to come back weeks and months later.

10. *Culture*. Cultural promotions and special events can significantly boost traffic for downtown's cultural venues, restaurants, galleries, crafts shops, specialty stores and boutiques — in other words, its cultural and restaurant niches. Sometimes special events can reassert the downtown's position as a place for the arts and history, when the downtown lacks a strong arts institution or building. While achieving these objectives, these cultural special events can also improve the downtown's appearance and attract new types of visitors to the area. The promotions and special events in this niche can be very diverse.

Many of the other events and promotions discussed in this chapter (for example, Riverfest in Red Bank, film festivals, the Cezanne exhibit, and food events) could also have been presented under the "culture" heading — remember, the niche in which a firm, event or promotion is placed often depends on how firms are being aggregated and what you want to do with them!

These events and promotions can vary considerably in their scale and cost. It may be a cliché, but big and expensive does not always mean better.

The Jazz Festival in Helena, MT. This nationally recognized jazz festival and parade has been in existence for over 15 years. A number of bands — 15 or more — play at seven downtown locations where people pay $50 for an all-event ticket. The bands also ride floats, horse-drawn wagons and other moveable stages in a musical parade through the downtown.[133]

Artwalk in Midland, MI. During this event the windows of over 60 downtown businesses are filled with a broad array of artworks that are integrated with other items in the window displays. This summer-long event ends with an Artwalk Celebration featuring special banners, visits to artists' studios, outdoor dance performances, music and free finger foods and candies.[134]

Gallery Walk in Raleigh, NC. After realizing that downtown had developed a niche of eight art galleries, local leaders decided to promote them by organizing a Gallery Walk. This simple promotion took place on one September Saturday evening, when all eight galleries agreed to stay open and invite people downtown to tour them. Each gallery provided refreshments for guests.

Sculpture in the Streets. The Sculpture in the Streets program of the Stamford [CT] Downtown Special Services District places between 20 and 25 pieces of monumental abstract sculptures along a prescribed, high-traffic route on the downtown's main streets. This innovative and major program costs over $65,500 to operate, and has the mission of presenting "Stamford Downtown as a regional cultural center where colossal outdoor sculptures created by renowned artists are exhibited in a busy urban environment attracting thousands of diverse patrons."[135]

Young Artists on the Avenue. This program in downtown Winnipeg, Manitoba brings youngsters downtown to exhibit their art works both in shop windows and along the sidewalks of Portage Avenue, the downtown's main street. Organized by a committee of the Downtown Business Improvement Zone, the event's original intent was to enliven empty storefronts with the work of professional artists. After a few years, it was discovered that young artists generated more excitement and brought more people downtown than the professionals. The event's organizers also believe that it will have a very important long-term positive effect: The youngsters will develop a positive orientation to the downtown that they will carry for the rest of their lives.[136]

11. *Ethnic Festivals.* Our nation's growing ethnic diversity has been well-noted in the media and it is demonstrated daily in our cuisine and restaurants. Today, such things as pizzas, bagels and salsa are as American as apple pie.

In some metropolitan areas, the number of ethnic groups has become staggering. But even relatively rural areas can have significant ethnic populations. When these groups are sufficiently large, they become niches, in effect, and offer rich market opportunities. In such instances, savvy downtown organizations can join with the appropriate ethnic organization and hold very successful festivals to penetrate this market. One of the advantages of such a partnership for the downtown organization is that it provides a built-in base audience. What the downtown organization can provide are organizational and promotional skills as well as the opportunity to attract a crossover audience. And while a foreign country may be at the heart of these festivals, ethnic events usually turn out to be marvelous, fun-filled celebrations of the local community.

Such festivals are usually built around food, but they also can (and should) contain parades, dancing, music, drama, religious displays, storytelling, crafts and games. The variety of activities offered increases a festival's attractiveness and helps assure its success; on the down side, however, having lots of activities increases a festival's scale and complexity, thus making it harder to organize and fund.

Many of these festivals become local institutions, with a number of them being celebrated for more than 30 or even 50 years.

San Jose, CA. This city is very ethnically diverse and has many festivals and events to celebrate this fact. For example, on every July 4th since 1991, the city has held a San Jose America Festival in which many ethnic groups — African, Greek, Vietnamese, and others — are brought together to provide a rich assortment of food, entertainment, arts and crafts. In 1994, the event drew over 300,000 visitors.[137]

The San Jose Downtown Association also helps to organize and promote a number of other ethnic festivals. Among them is the Vietnamese Mid-Autumn Festival which is partnered with the Viet-American Forum. In 1994, this event drew 15,000 visitors to a park adjacent to the downtown's Children's Discovery Museum. Local business and corporate sponsors help support the event, although modest admission fees have been added recently.[138] This is a children's festival which offers food, storytelling and children participating in an old Vietnamese tradition of parading in the evening with brightly colored lanterns.

The Cinco de Mayo Festival has been held in downtown San Jose for more than 15 years and draws in excess of 300,000 people. Sponsored by the American GI Forum, this festival features a big parade, entertainment on several stages, food booths, crafts and a major cultural display containing paintings, sculptures and photographs of Hispanic artists. There is also a "Sale-a-bration" sponsored by the Hispanic Chamber of Commerce. Local restaurants and retailers offer specials during the festival.[139]

Fergus, Ont. This Canadian community of just 8,000 people can draw over 35,000 on just one day of its three-day Fergus Scottish Festival and Highland Games. Celebrated for over 50 years, the festival is sponsored by the Fergus Chamber of Commerce and now has an annual budget of $300,000. In addition to the traditional Scottish "high tea," events include:

- a military tattoo patterned after the one in Edinburgh

- Highland games featuring the tossing of cabers and stones, and bagpipe and dancing competitions

- a traditional church service

- seminars on Scottish music and crafts

- a rugby tournament

Sacramento, CA. Here, the downtown district has joined with the Greek Orthodox Community to develop an annual Greek Food Festival. After being held for more than 30 years, the festival has developed a solid reputation that draws thousands of people to its food, music, cultural exhibits, dancing and religious displays. It is held in the downtown's Convention/Community Center.[140]

Chapter 6

Niches and Business

Recruitment Programs

A Growing Trend

Across the nation, more and more downtown organizations are creating and operating business recruitment programs. Such programs have long been one of the core components of the National Main Street Center's "four points" approach to the revitalization of small- and medium-sized downtowns. In recent years, larger downtowns, especially those with special districts — such as business improvement districts — have undertaken similar programs.

While most programs target retail tenant prospects (including entertainment), some are also concerned with office space.

A business recruitment program structured by a niche strategy is likely to be more focused and therefore more efficient and cost-effective. It also provides program objectives that stimulate aggressively proactive recruitment activities.

The Basic Idea

The overall goal of any business recruitment program is to help attract high-quality businesses. Such a program can be either passive or proactive.

1. *Passive Programs.* In a passive program, the downtown organization does not try to either identify or attract tenant prospects. The property owner or broker may bring a tenant prospect to the downtown organization, or the tenant prospect may present himself to the downtown organization. In either case, the downtown organization then tries to sell the prospect on leasing or buying in the downtown by providing information and facilitating such things as permits and approvals. Chambers of commerce have traditionally operated such programs when they have been actively involved in business recruitment.

Passive programs, since they typically do not give priority to one type of economic function over another, are almost antithetical to a niche strategy.

2. *Proactive Programs.* In a proactive program, the downtown organization works to establish close relationships with property owners in order to "educate" them about the types of quality tenants they can attract and to keep the downtown organization up to date on available properties. It also puts a considerable amount of effort into identifying tenant prospects and "communicating" with them by mail, phone or media advertising. The program puts an interested tenant prospect in contact with the property owners or brokers that have the types of commercial space the prospect requires. The downtown organization does not care which of these spaces a desirable prospect takes; its only goal is to maximize the chances of an attractive tenant prospect finding a suitable space somewhere in downtown.

A proactive recruitment program can be very advantageous for a downtown organization by:

- making it easier for property owners and brokers to get high quality tenants

- enabling the organization to encourage the implementation of its revitalization strategy

- increasing the probability that an attractive tenant prospect will find some appropriate location in the downtown

- allowing the organization to deal with red tape at an earlier stage of the recruitment process

While some proactive programs can be formulated independently of a niche strategy (they aggressively try to recruit any quality tenant), most proactive programs tend to adopt some kind of niche strategy, whether they are fully aware of it or not. Such a strategy helps programs become more efficient and effective by:

- narrowing the range of firms that need to be approached

- enabling a more focused sales campaign

- providing targeted information that can be used in the recruitment campaign

3. *Type of Professional in Charge of the Program*. Proactive programs vary in the *type of professional(s)* the downtown organization uses to make the outreach to landlords and/or tenant prospects. A few, such as Redbank, NJ, have brought in a developer because of the developer's network of contacts within the retail community and through such organizations as the International Council of Shopping Centers. Some others, such as the 34th Street Partnership, have brought in a real estate broker — again because of his network of contacts within the retail community and his knowledge of the district's commercial space. The broker's major function has been to identify property owners with significant amounts of available space and to help educate the Partnership about the types of retailers it might successfully pursue. However, most business recruitment programs do not use either brokers or developers, but instead rely on one or more staff members of the downtown organization.

4. *Impact of the Types of Businesses the Program Targets*. A recruitment program's specific characteristics will vary not only with the ambitiousness of its goals, but also according to the types of businesses it is trying to attract. For example, although many components of a downtown organization's retail recruitment program may overlap with its office recruitment efforts, many will not. The types of information tenant prospects require will differ: A retailer will be concerned about the characteristics of the trade area's residents, while a corporate office tenant prospect might be concerned about the labor shed, the availability of fiber optic cables and proximity to the airport. Moreover, there is much more information that is readily available (through personal networks or published information) about major retailers who are looking for space than there is about companies that are looking for office space. Similarly, within the retail area, the type of effort required to recruit major chains differs from that required to attract good "mom and pops." While a downtown organization may determine with relative ease the specific retail chains it wants to target and find out whether those chains are looking for space, it is a real challenge to identify independent merchants in other communities capable of adding luster to your downtown's retail mix, who also are willing to consider opening a shop there.

Basic Components of a Staff-Operated Retail Recruitment Program

The major components of a staff-operated proactive retail recruitment program (that is, one where the major tasks are performed by members of a downtown organization's or BID's staff) are described below. When appropriate, the discussion indicates components that brokers or developers might also use if they were involved in a downtown organization's recruitment program. Some benchmark indications of costs are provided, but care must be taken since a more reliable estimate of costs depends on the size and scope of a particular recruitment program.

1. *Publicizing Your Niche Strategy*. Once a downtown organization has completed its niche strategy it not only has a document that can give focus and direction to its activities, but also a potentially powerful public relations tool for promoting the downtown and attracting new businesses.

Experience has demonstrated that a strategy capable of projecting a compelling vision for a downtown and its niche(s), when well-publicized, can stimulate serious business prospects to come forward. For example, the formal adoption of a niche strategy by the Rutland Partnership and the large amount of press and TV coverage the strategy received helped to attract many important additions to that downtown's restaurant niche. And these new eateries tended to be of a unique nature, having style and distinction, such as Capers Bistro, The Coffee Exchange and Wine Room, Tapas, Mangiamo and Sweet Tomatoes Trattoria.

Many downtown organizations have on-staff people who are adept at placing stories with the local media. When this is the case, the cost of the public relations can be negligible, while the value of the media coverage can be enormous. If a downtown organization does not have a staff that is public relations-savvy, it can hire a consultant who is. Usually, the cost is affordable, and certainly less than what the organization would need to spend on advertisements to achieve the same level of market coverage.

An important potential downside to publicizing a niche strategy is that media reporters or editorialists may pan it. To avoid this situation, the downtown organization must develop good relationships with the media prior to launching the strategy. Having a competent public relations person on staff or hiring a consultant can help keep a downtown organization out of troubled waters.

2. *Establishing Good Contacts with Property Owners and Their Brokers*. This is an extremely important component of a successful retail recruitment program. Through these contacts the program can:

- find out about available commercial space

- gain enough trust and confidence to convince owners to make needed repairs and improvements

- have an opportunity to educate the owner about the downtown's retail niches, and inform them about competitive rents and leases

- have an opportunity to convince a property owner to hold out for a high-quality tenant in a targeted niche

These contacts are usually established by meeting with individual owners as well as with groups at meetings. The more owners there are, the more resources this task will take. The board of the downtown organization or downtown district will usually have the largest property owners on it. If it doesn't, that usually signals trouble for an organization.

Many downtowns complain about "snowbird" owners. If they live reasonably near to each other, it may be very practical for the downtown organization to spend $500 to $1,000 to send a high-level staff person out-of-state to visit and consult with the snowbird landlords.

This is a component on which most downtown retail recruitment programs encounter problems. For example, in Downtown X, NJ, the special improvement district's recruitment program successfully interested six major retail chains in one particular location, but the landlord refused to deal with their representatives "because they are brokers." In another downtown, a landlord refused to talk to a representative of a well-known coffee house chain "because chains are always hard to deal with and it takes forever to get a signed lease." You can avoid such situations by developing relationships between landlords and the downtown organization that are filled with trust and confidence.

A good starting point toward engendering this trust and confidence is to establish as a primary objective of the business recruitment program the provision of the type of assistance that will make it easier for landlords to get high-quality tenants in the targeted niches.

3. *Establishing a Database of Available Downtown Space.* This is essential to ensure that inquiries and responses to the program's outreach efforts can link tenant prospects to the most appropriate available spaces. The initial creation of the database can cost about $1,000 to $1,500. Updates,

which should be done on a continuous basis, should have negligible costs and be absorbed under standard staff operations.

The individual record in the database should identify the targeted niches for which the space is appropriate.

4. *Targeting Tenant Prospects.* The niches identified by the downtown organization's retail revitalization strategy indicates the type of retail activities the recruitment program should try to attract. This helps prevent falling into a "shotgun" program that is certain to waste resources and squander opportunities.

The method for identifying specific tenant prospects within each niche will vary depending upon whether they are chains or independents.

Retail Chains. Lists of retail chains in each niche can be easily assembled. Brokers and developers may know the people to contact at specific individual chains. They often also use published materials such as *Retail Lease Trac* and the *Retail Tenant Directory*; the former can also be obtained in PC- or MAC-readable form. Both provide information about retail chains that are looking for space, how much space they typically require and whether they are interested in downtown locations. They also provide the names, addresses and telephone numbers of the people to contact at each chain. Staff-operated retail recruitment programs are increasingly using these resources as well. For instance, the National Main Street Center has arranged to provide its members with *Retail Lease Trac* at a substantially reduced price. The cost of purchasing the raw data will probably be no more than $850, but as much as $2,000 or $2,500 may be needed to analyze the data and put them into a useful format.

A computer file version of *Retail Lease Trac* may contain as many as 1,200 listings. A niche strategy immediately identifies which listings will be of interest and quickly reduces the number that should be contacted.

In some downtowns, real estate brokers, landlords and other professionals may have personal contacts with retail chains. In such instances, it is a good idea to make them members of a business recruitment committee, to find out which contacts they have, and to ask them to personally communicate with their contacts in the targeted niches on behalf of the downtown organization.

Independents. From CD-ROM-based business databases, such as Select Phone, it is relatively easy to generate lists of independent retailers who are in targeted niches. Some of these databases will even provide the name of a contact person for each retailer. The problem is ascertaining how good an operation is and whether it would be an addition to your downtown. With retail chains, it is fairly easy to determine whether they are of the quality desired for your downtown because they have national or regional reputations. With independents it is more difficult to ascertain their quality without "shopping" them and finding out about their local reputations. Neither *Retail Lease Trac* nor the *Retail Tenant Directory* cover independent retailers, so finding out about those interested in moving or expanding requires direct communication with the owners.

Costs can easily get out of hand, so it is prudent to set a specific amount of money that can be spent on this task. This budget allocation should cover data costs, staff time (including field visits) and travel costs. One way to reduce costs and focus your search is to poll local businessmen — using focus groups or a survey — about independent retailers they would like to see recruited to their downtown.

5. *The Initial Outreach.* Besides brokers and developers, who may have personal connections, the initial contact with a targeted tenant prospect is usually made by sending a recruitment package.[141] This package usually contains a brochure or some other printed materials that "sell" the downtown, the trade area, the niche and last, but certainly not least, the site (see Figure 6.1). The package should contain the types of information that the retail site selector wants. This information can touch on the following areas:

- *The size and location of the site being offered.* In their initial communications with site selectors, downtown organizations sometimes forget to include some very basic information. A photo of the space being offered is also frequently useful (see Figure 6.2).

- *Who else is there and how well are they doing.* Knowing which retailers are in your downtown and which are located close to the site being offered is a key concern of site selectors. It is the first thing many of them will ask about. If there is a niche, it is a good idea to mention it and detail who is in it. Information on the downtown's retail sales overall and niche sales in particular can also be advantageously included.

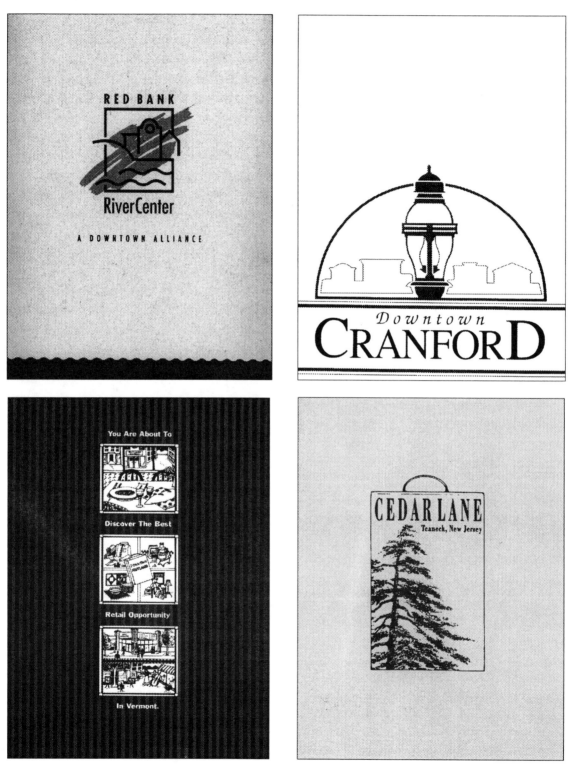

Figure 6.1

Cedar Lane Special Improvement District
Teaneck, New Jersey 07666

488 Cedar Lane

Size: 1,000 SF + fully sprinklered basement

Parking:

- On-street parking on both sides of Cedar Lane in front of store

- On-street parking on Alma Terrace behind store

- Three municipal lots with approximately 400 spaces within 300 feet of the store

Two Way 24 Hour Traffic Volume (Summer 1996): 16,900

Median Household Income in Teaneck 1995: $65,540

Contact:

Rob Holland, Kislak Realty — 908-750-3000

David Milder, Cedar Lane SID — 201-907-0493

Figure 6.2

- *Trade area information.* This can include a map of the trade area and data on its population size and demographics. Information about consumer expenditure potentials may also be useful. Remember that some retailers will have particular consumer groups that they are interested in, such as college students, the elderly or Latinos. Information about these groups should be provided (see Figures 6.3 and 6.4).

- *Potential customer traffic.* This can include information on automobile traffic counts and speeds. Increasingly, site selectors are learning to again appreciate high pedestrian counts.

- *Accessibility.* Including information on the amount and location of parking, the proximity to major highways and interstates and the presence of mass transit will be a necessity.

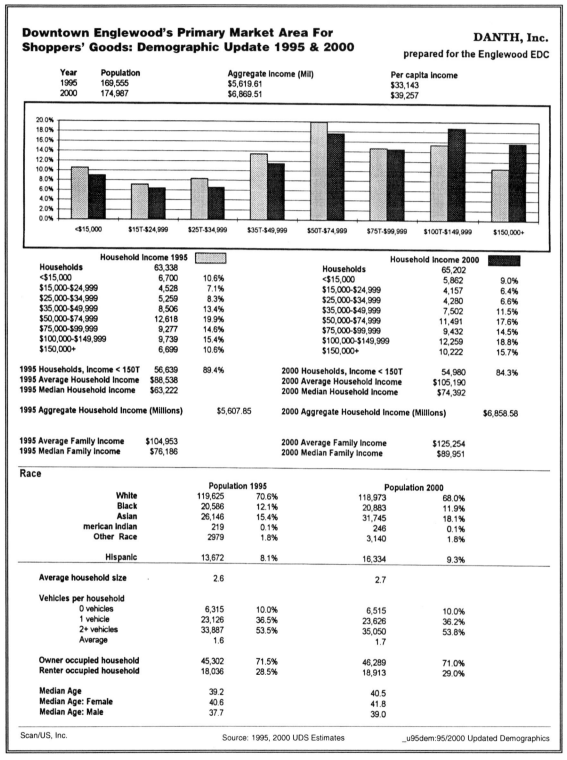

Downtown Englewood's Primary Market Area For Shoppers' Goods: Demographic Update 1995 & 2000

DANTH, Inc.

prepared for the Englewood EDC

Year	Population	Aggregate Income (Mil)	Per capita income
1995	169,555	$5,619.61	$33,143
2000	174,987	$6,869.51	$39,257

Household Income 1995			Household Income 2000		
Households	63,338		Households	65,202	
<$15,000	6,700	10.6%	<$15,000	5,862	9.0%
$15,000-$24,999	4,528	7.1%	$15,000-$24,999	4,157	6.4%
$25,000-$34,999	5,259	8.3%	$25,000-$34,999	4,280	6.6%
$35,000-$49,999	8,506	13.4%	$35,000-$49,999	7,502	11.5%
$50,000-$74,999	12,618	19.9%	$50,000-$74,999	11,491	17.6%
$75,000-$99,999	9,277	14.6%	$75,000-$99,999	9,432	14.5%
$100,000-$149,999	9,739	15.4%	$100,000-$149,999	12,259	18.8%
$150,000+	6,699	10.6%	$150,000+	10,222	15.7%

1995 Households, Income < 150T	56,639	89.4%	2000 Households, Income < 150T	54,980	84.3%
1995 Average Household Income	$88,538		2000 Average Household Income	$105,190	
1995 Median Household Income	$63,222		2000 Median Household Income	$74,392	

1995 Aggregate Household Income (Millions)		$5,607.85	2000 Aggregate Household Income (Millions)	$6,858.58

1995 Average Family Income	$104,953	2000 Average Family Income	$125,254
1995 Median Family Income	$76,186	2000 Median Family Income	$89,951

Race

	Population 1995		Population 2000	
White	119,625	70.6%	118,973	68.0%
Black	20,586	12.1%	20,883	11.9%
Asian	26,146	15.4%	31,745	18.1%
merican Indian	219	0.1%	246	0.1%
Other Race	2979	1.8%	3,140	1.8%
Hispanic	13,672	8.1%	16,334	9.3%

Average household size	2.6		2.7	
Vehicles per household				
0 vehicles	6,315	10.0%	6,515	10.0%
1 vehicle	23,126	36.5%	23,626	36.2%
2+ vehicles	33,887	53.5%	35,050	53.8%
Average	1.6		1.7	
Owner occupied household	45,302	71.5%	46,289	71.0%
Renter occupied household	18,036	28.5%	18,913	29.0%
Median Age	39.2		40.5	
Median Age: Female	40.6		41.8	
Median Age: Male	37.7		39.0	

Scan/US, Inc.	Source: 1995, 2000 UDS Estimates	_u95dem:95/2000 Updated Demographics

Figure 6.3

**Englewood's Primary Market Area For
Home Furnishings And Equipment:
Consumer Expenditure Potentials**

DANTH, Inc.
prepared for the Englewood EDC

1993 Households (Estimated)   63,278

	Expenditures per/HH	Comparison index	Annual expenditures (000)s
Refrigerators/Freezers	$52.23	111	$3,304.73
Washers/Dryers	$35.00	90	$2,214.79
Microwaves	$14.39	119	$910.43
Kitchen/Oth Appliance	$47.51	161	$3,006.45
Elec Kitchen Appliances	$18.78	118	$1,188.66
Vacuum Cleaners	$12.44	96	$787.38
Oth Hshld Appliances	$37.30	141	$2,360.51
Living/Dining Room Furn	$267.26	133	$16,911.43
Bedroom Furniture	$130.72	121	$8,271.99
Infants Furniture	$19.40	153	$1,227.40
Outdoor Furniture	$29.25	155	$1,850.85
Other Furniture	$82.00	148	$5,188.74
Carpeting/Rugs	$153.89	179	$9,737.74
Clocks/Lighting/Accessories	$111.21	121	$7,037.06
Storage Items	$3.49	113	$221.11
Leather/Travel Goods	$14.94	128	$945.11
Plastic Dinnerware	$1.43	77	$90.67
China/Oth Dinnerware	$18.19	140	$1,151.27
Flatware/Serving Pieces	$13.62	164	$861.64
Glassware	$10.54	172	$666.87
Cookware, Nonelectr	$9.74	106	$616.34
Window/Furniture Covers	$70.95	141	$4,489.78
Textiles, Bedroom Linens	$44.69	137	$2,827.76
Textiles, Oth Linens	$22.87	134	$1,447.11
		Total	$77,315.83

Reference Index: United States

Sources: 1993 Scan/US Estimates Based on Bureau of Labor Statistics Surveys, DANTH

Figure 6.4

- *Positive trends*. Include information showing that your downtown's economy is growing and that there are prospects for additional future growth. Information about physical improvements and capital investments can also be persuasive.

- *Attitudes towards business*. Retailers want to be assured that they will not have to spend too much time trying to cut local government red tape on permits, approvals, signage, etc.

This is a lot of information to convey. Experience suggests that the recruitment package should not try to exhaustively deliver all of it:

- Site selectors are very busy people and it is not a good idea to barrage them with too much information and "paper" in your initial contact.

- If site selectors are interested, they will contact you and request additional information. This gives the downtown organization another opportunity to make its pitch and to provide the desired data at the level of detail the site selector wants.

But, the downtown organization should be prepared to provide a wide range of information once a site selector expresses interest in a particular property.

The package should also summarize the downtown's major assets and invite the prospect to contact the downtown organization if he or she is interested in finding out about available properties or in obtaining more information about local markets, transportation, parking, and so on.

Another important objective of the package is to cultivate a positive image of the downtown in the prospect's mind, so that even if the prospect does not have an immediate space requirement, he or she might remember your downtown should such a need arise at a later date.

While a recruitment package can attempt to pitch just downtown as a location, a far stronger package will contain a one-page letter that focuses on the specific space being offered, describing its assets and appropriateness for that retailer. The letter also should offer to arrange a showing, to put the prospect in direct contact with the owner or to provide additional information.

The cost of the packages can vary considerably. A well-designed pocket folder with five inserts can cost about $10,000 for 500 folders. The cost per folder drops quickly on larger runs. A bare bones folder with just a logo might run about $1,500 for 500 folders — the inserts would be an additional cost, though they could be computer generated and run off on an as-needed basis. A more aspiring brochure, with four colors and more pages, can easily cost over $20,000.

Postage is another significant cost and, of course, will vary with the weight of the package and the number mailed. Another important cost is the manpower required to assemble, address and mail the packages. With proper supervision and a good system, this can be done by junior support staff.

Senior professional staff will be needed to put this component together. Staff time is a factor that is frequently overlooked when downtown organizations try to estimate the costs of developing and operating a business recruitment program.

6. *Following Up.* After the package is sent out, the prospect may reply, asking for more information or a showing. The downtown organization should then contact the appropriate property owner to arrange the showing. Someone fairly senior from the downtown organization should be present at the showing to sell the downtown, explain the permits and permissions process, and so on. It is also useful to have alternate spaces to show the prospect, should the first one not prove satisfactory. Participation in such showings can take a half-day of a senior staff person's time.

With a well-selected list of prospects, an attractive property to offer and a good-looking recruitment package, a mailing can get a response rate of about 10 percent.

But the most frequent result of a mailing is no response. Follow-up phone calls to gauge the prospect's level of interest are often useful. They do not need to be done by senior professionals; college students who are good on the phone are often more than adequate for this task. Completing 50 telephone follow-ups can take two weeks; at $10/hour, this costs $800 in support staff time.

Basic Components of a Staff-Operated Office Tenant Recruitment Program

In addition to attracting more retailers, a number of downtowns may also be interested in recruiting office-based businesses.

1. *Publicizing Your Niche Strategy.* As with retail recruitment, publicizing the office component of your downtown niche strategy can provoke serious

business prospects to come forward who are interested in one of the targeted niches. The same cautions are also relevant.

Questions arise as to whether or not the office and retail components should be woven together into one overall strategy and have just one release date, or should instead be separated and released independently within a few weeks of each other.

2. *Establishing Good Contacts with Property Owners and Their Brokers.* This component is the same as in the retail recruitment program and certainly of similar importance. If retail recruitment is also part of the program, it would just add more owners for the downtown organization or business improvement district to deal with. Its impact on costs would depend on how many additional owners would be added.

3. *Establishing a Database of Available Space.* Since the number of vacant offices in a downtown can be significantly larger than the number of vacant retail stores, the office database may be larger, cost more to create and cost more to maintain. In some downtowns, professional real estate service companies may track vacancies and make this information available for a fee.

4. *Targeting Tenant Prospects.* A niche approach can also help make an office recruitment program focused, efficient and effective.

To attract large corporations, it is important to contact their corporate real estate departments — if they have them.[142] However, in many large corporations the real locational decisions are made by the people in charge of specific operating units.

Small- and medium-sized companies are the type of office tenants that more and more downtowns are most likely to attract. Downtowns can find these companies by obtaining lists of firms in specific niche-related SIC categories from list houses or the CD-ROM business databases mentioned above. The problem is that none of these data sources can identify the firms that are looking for space.

For firms now officed in Manhattan, a real estate consulting service called Relocate can identify office tenants whose leases will soon expire. Similar services are emerging in other parts of the country. There is an annual cost for subscribing to such services.

Canvassing is another way of identifying "hot" tenant prospects for office space. For example, a few years ago over 1,800 small firms with offices in Midtown Manhattan were canvassed, with 627 telephone interviews completed. About 110 of the firms were moving within the next two years and 41 were judged to be good immediate tenant prospects for our client. Through canvassing, other firms were identified that should be targeted for the client's long-term campaign to cultivate tenant prospects. Canvassing can obtain the following types of information:

Firm 9101: Currently occupies 16,000 SF and has 60 employees; now pays between $16 and $25/SF; most concerned about the cost of new space and mass transit access; willing to relocate to Queens County; the CEO and top managers live in Queens, Nassau and Suffolk Counties; firm has many computer terminals and needs good electrical lines. On the seven key locational questions, had six positive answers.

The costs of canvassing can be significant. For instance, to contact 1,500 firms in the New York City metropolitan region — with the expectation of completing 500 telephone interviews — might cost $15,000. This might produce a hot prospect list of 50 to 100 firms.

5. *The Initial Outreach.* There is a very significant difference in the initial outreaches to large corporations and to small- and medium-sized companies. Large corporations are usually sent recruitment packages that have comparatively elaborate and expensive brochures, and at times resemble small four-color magazines. They can cost over $70,000. These elaborate packages can be heavy and their postage, consequently, can be significant. Large tenant prospects may also be provided information about specific buildings or spaces.

Smaller firms often are sent a more modest recruitment package that tries to sell the downtown as a business location, but generally does not offer the prospect a specific office space. The prospect is invited to contact the downtown organization for more information about available office spaces. Typically, the number of small- and medium-sized office tenant prospects contacted will be much larger than the number of retail prospects that the same downtown organization might contact. The reason is that the organization has less vital information about office tenant prospects than it does about retail prospects, especially with regard to who is looking for space and is willing to consider downtown locations.

6. *Following Up.* The downtown organization should follow up with office prospects that have responded to the initial mailing. As with the retailers, downtown should match prospects with appropriate spaces and arrange showings.

A telephone follow-up would be comparable to the canvassing described above in scope and cost, though it would not be as systematic.

Impact of Internet Web Sites

Having a Web site on the Internet may be an extremely important business recruitment tool in the future. This tool can allow business prospects to view photos, diagrams and data related to your space inventory or consumer markets at their own pace. They can then download what they are interested in. Conceivably, this can be a comparatively inexpensive way to disseminate lots of critical information.

One down side of this tool is the fact that from the perspective of the downtown organization, recruiting through a Web site is basically a passive strategy. Prospects who are searching for new business locations on the World Wide Web *must be able to find you*. A national survey of 750 Internet users conducted by Coopers & Lybrand found that most people found out about Web sites through old-fashioned word of mouth and that traditional media such as magazines, television and newspapers were still important sources.[143] This finding suggests that downtown organizations would be wise to retain more traditional channels of communicating with tenant prospects and to use their Web sites as a supplementary means of communications. The traditional communication channels can be used to inform prospects about the downtown organization's Web site address and describe what they will find there.

Another argument in favor of downtown organizations not relying too heavily and too fast on their Web sites as their primary business recruitment tool is the reality of how hard it is to efficiently search the Net. People who have used search tools such as Yahoo! or Alta Vista know that you get far more irrelevant "hits" than useful ones, and that weeding out the wheat from the chaff can be a very lengthy and tiresome process.[144] The situation is getting more difficult as more and more information becomes available on the Net. "If business people can't find critical information quickly, the Net's potential could be crippled."[145]

Let us also consider the fact that one of the major problems that downtowns have in recruiting new businesses is that many firms will not even give them a first look. Consequently, when such firms are browsing the Net they are not likely to either look for your downtown or to stop at your site if they inadvertently find it.

Another potential down side is the fact that many Web sites are either unattractive or provide useless and often banal information. There are reports, for example, that business site selectors "complain that data on the Internet is too inconsistent to make it a valuable tool."[146] A lousy Web site will broadcast a very negative impression of your downtown, just as a sloppy print publication would. Therefore, it is important that your Web site is well executed.

The Internet is also in great flux. Very significant new developments are expected over the next few years. Compared to the advances made in personal computers, the Internet is not even at the "386" stage.

It is prudent not to make an expensive investment that will soon be outdated by new technologies. Overall, the judicious way for a downtown organization to use the Internet would be:

- If you have the required funds, develop a Web site for your business recruitment activities.

- Register your site with as many Internet search tools as possible and think carefully about the words you use to identify it.

- Make sure your Web site is attractive and the information you provide is useful.

- Do not neglect your other means of communicating with tenant prospects until their lack of importance has been clearly demonstrated.

- In the near term, look to combine such things as mailings to make initial contacts with prospects and your Web site as a way for interested prospects to quickly obtain additional information and to express their interest in your downtown.

FOOTNOTES

[1]Soho stands for "south of Houston," an area in lower Manhattan filled with old loft buildings that has become a neighborhood where artists live and work.

[2]DANTH, Inc. et al., A Strategy to Reposition and Revitalize Garden City's Business Districts, Kew Gardens, NY: 1996.

[3]"Retail Action Strategies Based on Clustering and Recruitment," Downtown Idea Exchange, Dec. 1, 1990, pp.2-6; "Downtowns Cluster To Bolster Retailing Strength," Downtown Idea Exchange, May 15, 1991, pp.5-8.

[4]Leah Rickard and Jeanne Whalen, "Retail trails ethnic changes," Advertising Age, May 1, 1995, pp.1,41.

[5]"Like Totally Big Spenders," Business Week, June 3, 1996, p.8.

[6]Joshua Horwitz, "Retirees Seen as Benefit to Main Street Development," NYMSA Newsletter Spring 1991, p.8.

[7]Panel at the International Council of Shopping Centers (ICSC) conference in Las Vegas, May 1996.

[8]Anna Robaton, "Malls Add to N.Y. City's Retail Revival," Shopping Centers Today, June 1995, p.5.

[9]N. David Milder, Information on BID Retail Markets: Grand Central Partnership, Kew Gardens, NY: 1995, p.22.

[10]Ibid., p.23.

[11]New York Convention & Visitors Bureau, Inc., International Travel to New York City 1993, p.9.

[12]Panel at the ICSC conference in Las Vegas, May 1996. Merchants also like the tourist market because there are very few returns of merchandise.

[13]N. David Milder, A Retail Marketing Strategy for Downtown Rutland, Kew Gardens, NY: 1994, p.25.

[14]"Developing and Exploiting the Tourism Potential of Downtown," Downtown Idea Exchange, Nov. 15, 1993, pp.4-5.

[15]"Forgotten Downtown Becomes Year-Round Tourist Destination," Downtown Idea Exchange, Oct. 15, 1995, p.1.

[16]"Sociographics: Art Attack in America," Downtown Promotion Reporter, January 1996, p.6.

[17]Ibid.

[18]Office workers in Manhattan walk further on lunch time shopping trips than office workers in other downtowns, whose trips are usually under 1,000 feet.

[19]N. David Milder, Information on BID Retail Markets: Grand Central Partnership, Kew Gardens, NY: 1995, pp.9-21.

[20]DANTH associates, A Market Development Strategy for On-Street Retailing in Downtown White Plains, Kew Gardens, NY: 1995, p.31.

[21]See explanation of Soho in footnote 1.

[22]Jay Turner and Julie McKay, "Eureka Main Street: Cultural Arts Resource District," Main Street News, November 1995, p.3.

[23]Ibid.

[24]Robert Freedman, "Main Street Revitalization and the Arts: Peekskill Case Study—Part I," New York Main Street, Summer 1993, p.1.

[25]Confidential report to the Englewood EDC by DANTH, Inc. Estimate is based on data obtained from Scan/US.

[26]Waynesville also has a "sauerkraut" niche, its surrounding farmland having been a major supply source. Waynesville's three-day Ohio Sauerkraut Festival draws over 200,000 people. During the festival, Old Main Street is turned into one of the largest arts and crafts shows in the country, with more than 400 exhibitors.

[27]The name of this downtown is fictitious in order to protect the confidentiality of information given to the author.

[28]N. David Milder, A Retail Marketing Strategy for Downtown Rutland, Kew Gardens, NY: 1994, p.13.

[29]GAFO merchandise are those items sold in general merchandise stores (SIC 53), apparel and accessory stores (SIC 56), furniture and home furnishings stores (SIC 57) and other stores in the miscellaneous category (SIC 59).

[30]Ibid., p.14.

[31]"Bringing Supermarkets to Downtown and Making Them Work," Downtown Idea Exchange, April 15, 1996, p.5.

[32]Theodore Spitzer, "Maximizing the Benefits of Downtown Farmers' Markets," Center City Report, January/February 1991, pp.1,8.

[33]Zagat's survey found the Reading Terminal Market was the 15th most popular place to dine in the Philadelphia region. Zagat Survey 1996: Philadelphia Restaurants, New York: 1996, p.10.

[34]DANTH associates, A Market Development Strategy for On-Street Retailing in Downtown White Plains, Kew Gardens, NY: 1995, pp.49,62.

[35]Ibid., p.62.

[36]Ibid.

[37]Small office/home office; not to be confused with New York City's Soho neighborhood or other similar arts districts.

[38]Zagat Survey 1996: Philadelphia Restaurants, New York: 1996, p.10.

[39]Scan/US.

[40]Select Phone 1996.

[41]Zagat Survey 1996: Philadelphia Restaurants, New York: 1996, p.10.

[42]Bureau of Labor Statistics, U.S. Dept. of Labor, Consumer Expenditures in 1993, Report 885, December 1994, p.7.

[43]It appears that the importance of "the search for a meal" to downtown retailing may be affected little by size. For example, the Grand Central Partnership's survey of retailing in its business improvement district found 224 food service stores, or 31.6% of the total retailing. "Taking Stock," Shop Talk, Summer 1996, p.3.

[44]DANTH associates, A Market Development Strategy for On-Street Retailing in Downtown White Plains, Kew Gardens, NY: 1995.

[45]National Endowment for the Arts, "Research Note #38," 1993.

[46]Colorado Business Committee for the Arts, "The Economic Impact of the Arts in Metro Denver," 1993.

[47]The Port Authority of NY & NJ, et al., The Arts and an Industry: Their Economic Importance to the New York-New Jersey Metropolitan Region, New York: 1993, p.43.

[48]Ibid., pp.44-45.

[49]Ibid., p.51.

[50]"How to Build a Successful Outdoor Concert Series," Downtown Promotion Reporter, November 1995, pp.1-2.

[51]"Needed for Center: $13 Million and Faith," New York Times, pp.C11,C15.

[52]Information on Lincoln Road based on the author's field visit and "Culture and Art Drive Rebirth — and Rebuilding — on Lincoln Road," Downtown Idea Exchange, February 1, 1996, pp.6-7.

[53]Whether they are members of the Ballet or simply students at the ballet school, crowds of pedestrians are always watching them rehearse in the practice hall, which has storefront windows on Lincoln Road.

[54]"Arts Facility Will Anchor Downtown Santa Cruz," Downtown Idea Exchange, April 15, 1994, p.6.

[55]Ibid.

[56]"Downtown Becomes the Regional Art Center," Downtown Idea Exchange, Dec. 15, 1993, p.7.

[57]"All-America Downtowns," Downtown Idea Exchange, August 15, 1994, p.8.

[58]"The Arts: What's Really Popular," Downtown Promotion Reporter, December 1994, pp.9-10. This article discusses the NEA's report Arts Participation In America.

[59]DANTH associates, A Market Development Strategy for On-Street Retailing in Downtown White Plains, Kew Gardens, NY: 1995.

[60]Source: Downtown Research & Development Center, 1985.

[61]Ibid., also see footnote 5.

[62]Donald E. Hunter and Ernest E. Bleinberger, "Urban Entertainment Centers: Trends in Family Entertainment Go Downtown," PM Public Management, March 1996, pp.4-8.

[63]Urban Land Institute, "Project Reference File: Cocowalk, Coconut Grove, Florida," January-March 1993.

[64]Ibid., p.7.

[65]Carleton R. Meyers, "Attracting Factory Outlet Stores Can Spell Success for a Community," p.2.

[66]DANTH associates, A Market Development Strategy for On-Street Retailing in Downtown White Plains, Kew Gardens, NY: 1995, p.50.

[67]Kent Stasiowski and Seth Riseman, "Superstores Head Downtown," Urban Land, Dec. 1995, pp.33-38.

[68]Ibid., p.34.

[69]Ibid., p.35.

[70]Ibid., p.37.

[71]Telephone conversation, June 17,1996.

[72]"Wal-Mart's Road to Rutland Was a Downtown Route," Rutland Herald, April 26, 1996, p.4.

[73]"Downtown Stamford Seeks Chain Reaction," Crain's New York Business, August 21, 1995, p.22.

[74]Carleton Meyers, "Can Factory Outlets Revitalize YOUR Downtown?" p.14.

[75]"Can a Factory Outlet Store Work in Your Downtown?" Downtown Idea Exchange, August 15, 1996, pp.1,2.

[76]See the discussion on page 48 below.

[77]Claudia Deutsch, "Leasing Real Estate Space to Denizens of Cyberspace," The New York Times, Real Estate Section, May 26, 1996, p.7.

[78]Ibid.

[79]Ibid.

[80]"Telecommuting Centers: A New Way To Revitalize Downtown," Downtown Idea Exchange, August 15, 1994, p.5.

[81]Peter Siris quoted in "The Aging Baby Boomers," Barrons, March 11, 1991.

[82]"Value Retailing's Top Seven Questions," Value Retail News, October 1994, p13.

[83]Simmons Market Research Bureau, The New Affluent Lifestyles, New York: 1993, p.19.

[84]Ibid., p.11.

[85]Ibid., p.24.

[86]Ibid., p.27.

[87]"A Generation's Heritage: After the Boom, a Boomlet," The New York Times, February 12, 1995, pp.1,34.

[88]Regional Plan Association, "The Region Tomorrow: A Summary of Regional Plan Association's Economic and Demographic Projections to 2015," The New Century, Vol.1, No.1, April 1989, p.6.

[89]Regional Plan Association, "Outlook for the Tri-State Region Thru 2000," New York: 1987, p.7.

[90]Source: MAS national surveys in 1980, 1985 and 1990 of 10,000 shoppers.

[91]Dan Martin, "Shopping Trends," Planning, December 1990, pp.14-18.

[92]WWD Thursday, July 13, 1995.

[93]N. David Milder, "Ethnic/Minority Markets: A Key to Downtown Retail Success in the 1990s," Center City Report, Spring 1992, p.3.

[94]Estimates of the strength of this trend vary. On the high side Link Resources estimates that 41 million people work at home some time during the week and that 12 million work at home full time. Its forecasts are that one-third of the nation's workforce will be engaged in some kind of home-based work by the end of 1995. (See Center for The New West, Points West Chronicle, Spring 1994, p.5.) On the lower side, a survey by Find/SVP found only 9.1 million home workers in 1994. (See "Telecommuting Trends: Not as Many Home Workers as Thought," Downtown Idea Exchange, June 15, 1996, p.1.) In either case, futurists forecast no diminution in the growth of telecommuting for the foreseeable future; indeed, with the advent of easier-to-use, PC-based tele-conferencing, desktop conferencing and Internet technologies, there is likely to be further erosion of the need for businessmen to meet face to face. Thousands of others are setting up their firms in small offices located either at home or telework business centers.

[95]"California Is Reinventing Itself," Points West Chronicle, Spring/Summer 1996, p.1.

[96]Ibid., p.12.

[97]"Office Telecommuting Goes Long-Distance," The Washington Post, March 26, 1994.

[98]Philip M. Burgess, "Lone Eagles Are a Varied Species," The Rocky Mountain News, April 12, 1994.

[99]See footnote 1.

[100]The name of this downtown is fictitious in order to protect the confidentiality of information given to the author.

[101]Since the term "feasibility" is often associated with an analysis of a specific project's finances, the term "viability" will be used with regard to niches in this discussion. An assessment of a project's financial feasibility is more specific than the assessment of niche viability. Also, a number of projects could conceivably implement a niche strategy; if one is not financially feasible, another might be.

[102]"Rutland Cheers Arrival of Wal-Mart 'Smack in the Heart' of Downtown," Downtown Idea Exchange, July 1, 1996, pp.1-2.

[103]DANTH associates, A Market Development Strategy for On-Street Retailing in Downtown White Plains, Kew Gardens, NY: 1995.

[104]A real community here given an alias. See Table 4.2.

[105]See Office Worker Retail Spending, New York: International Council of Shopping Centers, 1988, and Lawrence O. Houstoun, Jr., "Nine Minutes To Retail," Urban Land, December 1989.

[106]"The Tourism-retail Connection," Downtown Idea Exchange, June 15, 1994, p.6.

[107]Ibid., p.7.

[108]Molly O'Neill, The New York Times, March 11, 1992.

[109]Ibid.

[110]This discussion will not be exhaustive, since it is not based on a large and systematic research effort, but on information the author has found in his day-to-day professional activities. Given the richness of the information uncovered, one can only wonder what a more systematic and arduous research effort might yield. The author invites readers to send him information about other successful niche marketing and promotional campaigns.

[111]Telephone conversation, October 16, 1996.

[112]Ibid.

[113]Telephone conversation, October 16, 1996. Downtown Port Chester, NY, the Manayunk commercial area in Philadelphia, the West End in Dallas and Old Pasadena in California are good examples of other downtowns where restaurant niches have become true destinations.

[114]Interview July 26,1996.

[115]"Decatur Organizes And Promotes Restaurants," Downtown Promotion Reporter, October 1995, p.4

[116]"New Shine for Diamond District," The New York Times, October 13, 1996.

[117]A process for creating the strategy that provides for extensive participation and input by niche business operators can be a good way of educating them and mobilizing their support. The insular operators, almost by definition, are not likely to participate in such a process. The process is most likely to have a positive impact on those having zero sum market perceptions.

[118]Robert W. Ohlerking and N. David Milder, "Briefing Paper: Retail Advertising and Promotions," Kew Gardens, NY: 1995, DANTH, Inc., p.4.

[119]Peter Beronio, "Briefing Paper: Garden City Promotions: Special Events," Kew Gardens, NY: 1995, DANTH, Inc., p.8.

[120]Bulk delivery at drop-off points.

[121]Glenn Collins, "Advertising: Manhattan museums pool resources for a newspaper campaign," The New York Times, July 19, 1996.

[122]Ibid.

[123]The material discussed in this section is based on information obtained from a panel on tourism held at the ICSC conference in Las Vegas, May 5-9, 1996.

[124]"Food, Glorious Food! Or What's Cooking Downtown," Downtown Promotion Reporter, October 1995, pp.1-5.

[125]Ibid.

[126]Ibid.

[127]Ibid.

[128]"Make the Most of Downtown Cinema with a 'Late Show' Promotion," Downtown Promotion Reporter, August 1995, p.10.

[129]"Downtown Appreciates Its Employees, and Their Business," Downtown Promotion Reporter, April 1995, p.7.

[130]"World's Largest Office Party," Downtown Promotion Reporter, February 1991.

[131]"Exciting Benefits for Downtown Workers," Downtown Promotion Reporter, November 1993, p.10.

[132]"The Car Culture Brings a New and Appreciative Audience Downtown," Downtown Promotion Reporter, February 1996, pp.1-4.

[133]"Great Festivals & Parades Require Good Planning and Management," Downtown Promotion Reporter, September 1993, p.8.

[134]"Artwalk Brings Beauty — and People — Downtown," Downtown Promotion Reporter, March 1995, p.5.

[135]"How To Paint the Town with Downtown Arts Events and Promotions," Downtown Promotion Reporter, May 1996, pp.3-4.

[136]Ibid., pp.1-2.

[137]"From Cinco de Mayo to a Vietnamese Mid-Autumn Festival." Downtown Promotion Reporter, January 1, 1995, pp.1-2.

[138]Ibid., p.2.

[139]Ibid. p.2.

[140]"Partners Promote Souvlaki Downtown," Downtown Promotion Reporter, December 1993, p.2.

[141]And the brokers and developers will often use a similar package as follow-up even when they do have a personal contact.

[142]The National Association of Corporate Real Estate Executives' (NACORE) membership directory is very helpful.

[143]"Untangling the Web," Business Week, July 29, 1996, p.6.

[144]"The Ultimate Indexing Job," Business Week, August 12, 1996.

[145]Ibid. The National Center for Supercomputing Applications has put a supercomputer to work to develop an indexing scheme that can solve this problem. The solution is not expected to be found any time soon.

[146]See "Who's Surfing Downtown on the Internet," Downtown Idea Exchange, August 1, 1996, p.1.